Friendship Street

Stories from 1950's

J M BARRY

Preface

The 1950's were years of change. For some of the people who lived in the cities of America life was structured around separated immigrant or ethnic cultures that settled during the influxes and immigrations of the late 19th and early 20th centuries. Herein are stories of a neighborhood of such poor and working class people who had no way out, who did not participate in the emerging economy and good times of the post war era. Their lives were fixed and stagnant; they lived day to day, change unreachable for most of them, surviving in a community of limited possibilities. Yet they continued, with hope, faith, and a few bright moments.

About The Stories

 Rage ... describes an attitude existent in all the stories from the neighborhood of Friendship Street.

The Bald Lady and her Husband ...incorporates the nature of life in poor communities when crisis enters.

The Kid Who Got Killed ...is about compassion, especially from kids who are touched by neighborhood sorrow.

The First Rock ...shows the struggles and bias in leaving the neighborhood.

The Summer Party ...shows the callous attitudes undercurrent in even a simple experience like a well-intentioned party.

They Didn't Let Chappie Join the Army ... a long story about one man's struggle to find his place and himself in the tensions of changing times.

Survival and Saying Goodbye ...a story about an unfortunate experience, change and moving forward.

A Neighborhood is defined by the author's experiences.

Rage

"Stay away from those places," we were warned. My Grandmother, our Nana, was fearful for us and made us fearful. We were newcomers on Friendship Street , a family fallen on hard times, a family on the downslide when much of the society around us was moving up. My parents scrunched a family of six into a two room studio apartment in the basement of a made over mansion on Friendship Street.

We stayed away from the Greeks because they were different, and from the Italians and the Black areas because we were different. We were Irish mostly and a little bit French. We didn't belong on Friendship Street. We didn't belong anywhere really. We knew our place was to keep our distance, and on Sunday mornings to go to mass at Irish St. Michael's and not the downtown Cathedral.

We lived on a section of Friendship Street that was in the Catholic Cathedral parish. That didn't matter to our Nana. Our Great Grandfather Tom was one of the founding parishioners of St. Michaels's RC, laid some of the brick, and installed the boiler that heated the great church. It didn't matter that our father couldn't find us a tenement in St. Michael's. That was our place. For a long while our Nana wouldn't visit us on Friendship Street. To do so would have been disloyal to the principals she held. The Irish didn't move down they moved up. We had moved down.

Our block wasn't as bad as some; the houses were less run down. There were fewer bars or bad places as our Nana called them. Friendship Street wasn't a part of our old Irish neighborhood where the Murphy's had lived since 1895, all of our Nana's lifetime, and all of our Mother's lifetime until she had to leave Pavilion Avenue. My Mother and Dad and the kids lived on the avenue until I was twelve years old, until the house we rented had to be given up.

When World War II ended and housing became scarce the house we rented was needed for the brother of the landlord, a returning soldier and his family. My Dad wasn't in the army, so he had no standing when it came to keeping the house for his family. It was one more strike our Nana made on the list of deficits he had. Before Friendship Street we lived just five houses up from the Murphy Mansion, the neighborhood label for the stalwart three floored cottage that my Great Grandmother Murphy bought at in 1895. Her name was Lizzie; everyone called her that when she was talked about. Lizzie cobbled together some savings from the weekly housekeeping money my Great Grandfather gave her to run the house. Lizzie came from a landed family in Ireland, and her family pride made her drive my Great Grandfather Tom Murphy to buy the house once she'd saved enough for the down payment. Tom wasn't happy at the thought of his wife deceiving him.

"If you didn't need all the housekeeping why did you take

it?" He asked as they stood at the front of the house as it was auctioned to the highest bidder, my Great Grandmother.

The Murphy Mansion was the center of the world for the family and was to be so for the extended family for the next eighty years. It was a place to go if you needed help, or wanted to be comforted; the door was always open. One never knew who might be sleeping in the spare room, one person or a family crowded in. There was always room, always enough food. I remember my mother and her four kids crowding in on Nana for a time when our Dad, beaten down with alcohol, debt and despair, left us. We stayed at the Murphy Mansion for a while, until things could be returned to near normal.

Despite my Great Grandfather Tom's balking at the auction sale he grew proud of his family home. Lizzie died young, in her early 40's, from cancer. He made the house her shrine. He kept her clothes in his closet, her perfume on the dresser, her photos displayed for all to see, and her piano that used to ring with joy covered and silent, as if he were waiting for her to return to play it. He nurtured her flower gardens, tended her grape arbor, and painted the house every spring, fresh in the colors she'd chosen; nothing was changed.

The house had gas jets for light, but in the 1930's, when all the houses around had been converted to electricity, the Murphy Mansion had to give up the gas jets. Tom was adamant; no change!

His grown sons arranged a visit for Tom to his sister's home in Brooklyn, not telling him about the work electrifying the house. When he returned to find the house electrified he was furious and remained so for some months to follow. He decided, after a fashion, that Lizzie would have liked electricity. He prayed for her and he talked to her every day as if she was still with him, and in a way she was. His conversations with her helped him accept change. We were less eager about change, about moving away from Tom's world, Lizzie's world that nurtured us long after they died.

We moved to Friendship Street, a long step down from the working and middle class Irish neighborhood of my early years. The landscape of the new neighborhood was defined by where my sister and I could not go more than where we could. A four block area around Dick Loving's apartment house was the extent of our world, except for the long walk to the out of district school. My mother used Nana's address to keep us in our old school. As I grew older I found my way beyond the constraints and limitations of the neighborhood into the expanded world. I was twelve years old when we moved to Friendship Street and seventeen when we left to move up again. It was a time during which my inner soul was ruled by anger and a sense of injustice.

The main block in front of our house near Friendship Street School was at the edge of my boundaries. Dirty Gertie lived across the street in a small cottage a little worse for wear. She had one of the hardest stories in the neighborhood. On one day Gertie's plight spurred a sense of social injustice unknown on the street before the welfare department sent the cops out to take her youngest kids away. Gertie had ten kids, mostly with different fathers. My band of friends and I were too young to know the morality issues that fanned the action against Gertie at the time. Wrongness for us was the cop Carmody who beat his kids and wife, or the owners of the falling down houses who charged too much rent and didn't fix the doors and windows, or the evil lady who ran the local thrift shop and sold used house wares and clothing too expensively and alluded to most of her customers as bad people, all alcoholics and ne'er do wells. I didn't think alcoholics were bad, just drunk. Like my father who some weeks spent his whole paycheck getting drunk. He wasn't bad. I wasn't sure what she meant by ne'er do wells, except maybe all of us who were too poor through no fault of our own except not having enough money.

The outrage about Gertie's kids spread around the neighborhood. Gertie took good care of her kids. She kept them clean. They weren't in trouble, none of them. They went to catechism on Wednesday's after school like all of us in that mostly Catholic neighborhood, except for the Methodists who ran the thrift shop on Broad Street, or the Episcopalians who owned the big apartment house next to Loving's where I lived. Gertie let the older neighborhood girls pull her babies around the block in their wagon.

When the cops came to Gertie's place the word spread and people came out of their apartments and flats to watch. The grownups for the most part stood silent, watching. The kids yelled and from the back of the gathering a few expletives salted the general rumble. Nobody said the f word then, or maybe even thought it. In some ways it was a more innocent time.

Some of us cried. Our outrage was fanned by Gertie's shrieks as her kids were put into the back of two patrol cars, two of the babies in the arms of a gray woman, gray hair, gray dress, gray face, who did nothing to comfort the screaming that wailed out of their tiny faces. They wailed and wailed until all of us in our group were crying, sniffing back sobs and stifling the sick feeling from tightened bellies that witnessed what could happen to any of us. We were vulnerable: young, ten, eleven, twelve years old, young enough to be fearful and old enough to recognize the reality of the cracked glass of our collective lives.

Rage welled up, churning, fueled by exaggerated imaginings of what would happen to Gertie's kids. Maybe they'd be sent to the reform school where they'd be beaten daily. Maybe they'd be given to some family out in the suburbs as foster kids or even adopted. Maybe they'd never see their mothers again. That was bittersweet. The fear of loss and the hope for redemption were the two faces of life on Friendship Street. Not one of the band of us kids that hung together had not experienced the buoyant hope, the contraband thought: we might be rescued and swooped off to some other place; we might go where kids played ball or sailed boats on the nearby bay or joined scouts or had beds, or yes, whole rooms to themselves. I might go to Nana's and live with her. But that meant loss and pain. The hopes were stifled guiltily. As the day turned into evening and the hot humid air of the summer hung over the street, our small band gathered together as darkness set in. We mingled by the school, watchful eyes on Gertie's house, murmuring anger, whispering for justice.

The silence of the night was shattered with crashing glass. Rage threw the first rock and the next and the next. Then the contest took over, the competition to see how many panes of glass each could break in the yellow stone former primary school building that now housed the welfare office. Mrs. Rafferty screamed out her upstairs apartment window at the noise. It was late, after ten and dark. The shades were drawn on most of the windows until Mrs. Rafferty lifted her dark green roll up shade and shouted into the night to the miscreants abroad to cease and desist from making such a racket. There was no illusion she cared about the windows or the school building. She didn't. She'd never seen the inside of a school herself, and her grown kids had almost as perfect a record, bunking as much as possible before being thrown out at the legal age of fifteen to go to work. Sirens cut through the joy and glass. We fanned out across the blocks to our various homes.

It was morning before the real damage could be assessed and the shards of glass like crystal borders gleamed across the front of the building in the bright day's sun. Rage subdued, we went to watch the investigation. Some of the bunch stayed back, across the street. I was bolder.

"Don't go there," they tugged at my sleeve. I was eternally curious. My survival depended upon it.

"Hey, whadaya know about this mess?" The policeman was not a stranger to our neighborhood. He wasn't the usual beat cop. He came out if there were special problems, like every pane of glass on one side of the welfare building smashed.

I shrugged. He reached toward me and put his large hand across the top of my blond head and mussed my hair around. I stood almost to his armpit as his fat arm held me. "Some mess, huh?"

"Some mess," I answered.

"What the hell would make anyone do this?"

I shrugged. "Dunno."

"Hey, girlie," he smiled, "you'd better get back across the street before you get cut."

In my heart I wanted to rage, to shout and let him know why, and let them know, all of them, whoever they were, that Billy Carmody had thrown the first rock, and I threw the second, the rock he put into my fist, my initiation. But prudence kept me and

Billy safe. It wouldn't always, but at that time and in that place it did.

The rage was always there on Friendship Street, just under the surface, just below the second layer of skin. Sometimes it broke through. Then it was beat back, stamped down, pushed into a dark corner where it gnawed and festered. It almost never won out and went furiously forward shouting for overlooked dignity with appropriate outrage for change that never came.

Dirty Gertie got her kids back in a few days without any fanfare of general outcries of joy. There was a sense that there would be other takings on other days, and an awareness that hope had flown for each of those little people. They came back to her large wide arms that squeezed them with love and smacked them with frustration.

The Bald Lady and Her Husband

The bald lady and her husband were tenants on the second floor back of Dick Loving's apartment building on Friendship Street. Not known to the other tenants or neighbors but carried by the gossip wind it was said they were desperately lonely and struggled daily with her long term illness. There was all manner of speculation about why she was bald. It was a bad thyroid; that was the generous decision. Somebody's daughter had a bad thyroid many years before and kept taking medication without ever seeing a doctor and all her hair fell out. Other thoughts, the mean gossip: maybe it was syphilis or one of those other horrid contagious diseases. Who cared anyway? Too bad she couldn't afford a better wig. The reddish one she had, cut short, didn't do a thing for her. She had a pretty face and nice figure. Too bad.

They were a couple isolated from the neighborhood. They didn't have children. It made them suspect in a community, if you could call it that, where people scraped to get by because they had kids, sometimes too many. People warned their kids off from going into their apartment, not that they'd ever been invited. It was a taboo. The mysterious couple was off limits. They lived in the building within their own circle, no friends or family visiting, not attending to the people or things around them, never mind not weaving their lives into the warp of the building. They came and went every day with little notice of others. They went to work; nobody knew where. He, nobody knew his name, wore a clean pressed gray mechanics

coverall, everyday a fresh one. Not like the other men who poured themselves day after day into heavy overalls that could stand on their own with the strength of the oil and grease imbedded in their fibers. She, somebody said her name was Marge, went out every day with a pretty skirt and a starched blouse, like you'd wear in an office, and hose neat with seams straight, and a neat handbag and a small sack with her lunch, and her wig neatly place and tied under a scarf on cold days. On warms days she wore a net chiffon scarf, always a scarf, as if to hold the wig in place against a wild wind.
It was easy enough for them to be so well turned out, with no kids to iron and wash for, that was the neighborhood gossip.

There was nothing about them that gave them entry into the world around them until the night Jenny's two year old brother ate the pills, gentian of violet, that the doctor prescribed for Jenny's foot infection. Jenny was twelve then. She and her family, mother and father, older sister and ten year old and two year old brothers, lived in the two room basement apartment. Dick Loving thought the couple just had the baby when he rented the apartment to them. The older kids lived with a grandmother until one by one they appeared. He let the family use the extra room in the back of the unfinished part of the basement for storage and laundry lines. He let Jenny and the little boy keep toys in the front part of the basement, and gave Jenny the use of the unused whitewashed coal bin so she could do her homework in a quiet space.

That night Jenny's mother was working the 3 to ll shift at the rubber plant. It was after ten o'clock and her father left for the midnight shift at the railroad yard. Her older sister had not come home yet from her friend's house. It was like every other night. Jenny was asleep on the daybed in the combination living room kitchen when they baby's scream woke her. The brilliant purple dribbling down from his mouth told the story. The voice of the doctor rang through her brain.

"You be sure to keep these pills high up away from the baby. They are poisonous."

The night became a blur. Jenny grabbed the baby and his blanket and ran through the cellar and up the stairs to Harry and Kay's place on the first floor. They didn't answer as she beat against the door. She raced through the back entry way outside and screamed up at the windows of the house next door. The Carmody's lights were on.

"What's all the ruckus?" Mrs. Carmody shouted out the upstairs window.

"The baby ate poison," Jenny screamed.
"Where's your mother?" Mrs. Carmody called down. She knew. Why was Jenny waking up the whole neighborhood? She didn't ask it but it was her question.

Jenny's Sister Lois appeared and pulled the baby from her. Harry and Kay emerged, she in her red chenille robe, he in his light blue boxer shorts and undershirt. Jenny stared at them, all staring back, nobody moving, nobody sure what to do.

Jenny left the baby with Lois and raced by Harry and Kay up the back stairs to the second floor and pounded on the door. The husband opened it, still in his slacks and a white dress shirt. His wife came from behind him, wrapped in a silk flowered robe, her head uncovered, and across the room on a stand, the wig like an independent life form stood prominently.

"The baby ate poison!" Jenny screamed.

The man reached out to the girl and put his hand on Jenny's shoulder.

"I'll get my keys," he said after she blurted out the story. He followed the distraught young girl down the stairs. The lady followed after a few minutes, having slipped into a skirt and sweater, the wig slightly askew atop her head. She gently took the baby from Lois trying to calm the screaming little one.

"Let's go to the hospital," she said.

"We don't have any money," Lois cried.

The lady knew. There was no money for things like sickness or dying on Friendship Street.

"Somebody call my mother," Lois sobbed to no one in particular.

"We have to go," the woman said. She turned with the baby and she caught hold of Jenny's hand. "Let's go," she said. "Help me with your brother."

Lois, crying, was left with Harry and Kay to take care of her ten year old brother. A cab drove up as the man bundled the lady, Jenny and the baby into his car.

"Who's gonna pay me?" the cabbie asked. It was the last thing they heard before they drove away.

Jenny looked back at the jumble of sleepy people standing at the side of the house bewildered and gossiping. Kay was holding Lois in her arms patting her head. The younger brother, in his pajamas, was just emerging down the alley and Mr. Carmody picked him up in his fat arms. As the car drove around the corner a squad car raced down the street, siren blaring.

"That must be for us," the woman said. She was in the back seat comforting Jenny's two year old brother who had finally stopped screeching. She had a towel and was wiping the purple spittle from his around his mouth and tongue.

"We're not going back," the man answered.

"Of course not," She reached across to Jenny and patted her thigh. "He'll be okay."

"He ate poison," Jenny answered, "He's going to die."

"Shush," she said, "he'll be fine." Her wig was still a bit akimbo. It didn't matter. Her eyes were a brilliant blue and her warm lips and soft skin were young, though Jenny thought she was her mother's age. She was pretty, Jenny thought to herself, the way her mother would be pretty if she didn't have four kids and a drunken husband and a factory job in the middle of the night.

The hospital yard was busy with ambulances and cars carrying people in similar crises. Young Jenny clutched her brother's hand as she got out of the car. The man took her little brother from her.

"Let me have him," he said, "he's heavy for you."

They walked into bright lights and were whisked in a sweeping movement down the corridor and into a room with instruments and mirrors. Jenny grabbed at her baby brother, and the woman and a man in a white uniform pulled her away.

"He'll be fine," the man said. "You come out here in this room and wait."

"I'll stay with him," the woman said.

It was a long time before they came back. So long that Jenny was sure he died. She sat on a long tan colored plastic couch and slipped into half-sleep.

"I told you to put that medicine away." Her mother's voice jolted Jenny awake. She was there, finally. Jenny reached out to her mother who put her arms around her daughter.

"He's okay," she said. "They pumped out his stomach. Poor little guy."

Jenny felt bad and her mother made her feel worse describing in detail the procedures used to bring the poison pills up from the baby's stomach. Jenny knew she'd let her mother down. The woman with the wig came and stepped between mother and daughter.

"Sit down," she said to the mother. "I'll get you some tea." She turned to Jenny. "I'll bring you some too."

The tea was warm and the three of them waited until a nurse came for Jenny's mother. She had to fill out forms. A fear began to fill Jenny as recalled her sister's frantic pleading. There wasn't any money. Jenny felt her stomach clenching. What do you do when you don't have money? Would they have to go to jail? Would they take her father or mother away? The woman sat beside the distraught girl and reached her arm around her shoulder as her mother got up and followed the nurse.

"We don't have any money," Jenny said.

"It's all right," she answered. "Sometimes you don't need money, when it's an emergency."

"I'm sorry I woke you up," Jenny lied to her.

"You didn't," she answered. "I was reading. I'm glad we could help."

A myriad of visions moved in and out of Jenny's dream world later, when they went home and she finally got to sleep.

"I'm not waking you up for school," her mother said.

Jenny didn't resist as she usually did if her mother kept her out of school to watch the baby if she had an appointment or had to work an extra shift. She buried herself under the blanket and was asleep before her sister slipped into the bed beside her. The dreams reflected her fears, of her brother's face turned permanently purple, of police cars chasing, and Jenny in the front running, holding her brother, her mother's blaming, the white casket that faded into sunlight, and there, in the midst of it, the lady with the soft face, warm smile, and wig akimbo smiled through.

The gossip on the back stoop and the front porch and across the street went on for a time and exaggerated the proportions of the episode. It was blended into the mythology of the neighborhood, and after a while was tucked back into a corner. The baby was an oddity until the remnants of the purple faded from his face, and scoops of ice cream or lollipops stopped coming in his direction from the local storekeepers who shared the comforting and recognized the story had a happy ending.

Life continued. The man and woman came and went day after day, not acknowledged for their quickness to respond. But there was a small change, a smile passing now and again between the neighbors as they passed by.

Two weeks later Jenny returned from school and went into the back entry; there was a small package with her name on it. She took it down the back stairs into the kitchen. Her father and mother were both getting ready to leave for work. They were both working swing shifts, four to midnight now that Jenny and her sister were old enough to take care of the boys. They liked working the same shift and made more money that way.

"Your sister isn't home from school yet," Jenny's mother said.

Jenny knew. Lois walked home ahead of her and signaled when she turned into her friend Ann's house. She'd be stopping there for a while. She knew Jenny would go straight home

"She's probably had to stay after school," her mother lied to herself. She knew like Jenny knew that there was no routine for Lois. "I left the dinner in the fridge."

Jenny knew. She always left the dinner made. She took care of her kids. She loved them. Her father was tying his work shoes, black and wrinkled from too long use."We can count on you," he said and smiled a pained smile. They all knew.

"I got a package," Jenny said. She took the brown paper wrapping off it. There was a note: "For your courage and good sense. Good luck, Marge and Paul. The upstairs people."

There were three books inside. Mark Twain's Tom Sawyer; an autobiography of Susan Blackwell, the first female doctor in America; and a book of stories for small children.

"That's nice," her father said.

"Nice to have money enough to buy books," her mother said sharply, embarrassed by the whole event and wanting it past and done.

Jenny cherished the books. She read the stories to her little brother over and over. It was a special time for them when they sat on the day bed or the floor and read the stories. Jenny went up the backstairs later in the week to knock on the door and to say thank you. Her courage failed. She stood, hoping before she knocked they would open the door, that they would sense her being there and know how much she wanted to reach into the kindness of their lives and say thank you. She heard their noises, the soft sound of voices, not raised in anger, the hum of music from the radio. Her hand failed. She retreated to her small library in the cellar coal bin and penned a thank you note and drew a picture of the man carrying her brother and the woman, her wig on straight, standing beside him and Jenny beside her. It was a dream that looked like a real together family. It was a dream of visions possible. She tucked the note into their mailbox. That was all.

The couple continued on with their routine for a while longer and one day they were gone. They moved. There was a burst of final gossip about them. There was mystery about them. It was never solved in a neighborhood that feared differences.

The Kid Who Got Killed

The news spread like wildfire flamed by the fuel of the bored, the dull, the prayer-good people chastened by life who wished their lot was not the worst. Like my grandmother said, eternal optimist that she was, there were always those worse off than we were.

Kids and grownups emerged from yards along the street, from stores where they were shopping responding to the shouts of "a kid got killed on Agnes Street. Run over by a truck." I was roller-skating on the sidewalk doing figure eight turns in my best twelve-year-old form, working to keep the clamp skates from tearing the soles off my shoes. There was something going on. People were staring down the street, moving from their steps and piazzas in the direction of Prairie Avenue. I pulled the skates off my feet and threw them under the steps so they wouldn't get stolen and followed after the assembling curious crowd. The small parade turned the corner from Friendship onto Agnes where two blocks down a fire truck and a police car were in the middle of the street on either side of the large coal truck. In the offing a wail of the ambulance sounded from the direction of Rhode Island hospital.

The less adventurous of us slowed. Some cluttered around the scene. McNair, the beat cop, was urging the crowd back.

"Give 'em room. Get back." No point telling them to go home.

It was a big coal truck, the cab black and the rest of the truck covered with coal dust black. It was always in the neighborhood. It was slow and it was easy to grab onto the sides or back and get a ride on your skates or hold on and lift your legs. For the thrill of it before the driver waved his arm out the window and shouted, sometimes swore, and a kid had to jump down or let go. By the time he stopped the truck the kids were gone, barreling down the street or cutting into an alley.

"He hated the kids," someone damned the poor man.

"The kid's head is crushed like a melon!" another said.

My stomach churned. The image flashed of a dropped melon on the concrete floor of the Friday night market at Hoyle Square split open in thirds, its juicy orange substance tumbling over its yellow and white casing; it brought me to a stop. Was that what spilt brain looked like?

The driver was hunched over, his shoulders convulsing, his body sobbing. For once I was comforted by McNair's shouts.

"You people go home!" he yelled, the twinge of Irish brogue resonating.

I moved back about a block and sat down on the curb, away from the energy that clamored around the poor dead kid.

The kid lived in the old brown apartment house on Early Street called "Early Arms". Long since the two wings of the four-storied clapboard structure gave up standing straight. They loomed, tilting a little, patched with different shades of brown paint. Clotheslines sagged from pulleys on the kitchen windows running back to the trees at the far end of the lot. It wasn't a yard. It was a dirt pathway between it and the other houses crowded around it. The trees, bare in winter, held their branches up, arms for the sole purpose of holding laundry lines. No self-respecting bird would take up residence in the brown house trees.

The building, like so many of the tenements around it, held far more families than was its original plan. The flats were cut into two or sometimes three smaller apartments. It wasn't cheaper to rent one of the places. Up near Broad Street the flats rented for less a month than the apartments. But on Friendship Street the rents were paid weekly, and if you were late, well, you'd slide by and make it up when you could. The owners didn't lose. They charged a late fee, sometimes five dollars my father said. The families on Friendship weren't smaller. Just crowded and poor. The apartments on Early and Agnes were some of the worst.

"She got cut off welfare. Now her kid is gone," somebody said about the Mother.

"I never seen her."

"I wouldn't know her if I did."

"Was she in the parish?"

"The kid was always chasing the trucks."

"Stupid kid."

"Don't speak evil of the dead."

"Poor woman."

The sounds permeated my dizzy brain. Just this morning everything was normal and the kid was alive and hadn't chased the truck and jumped on and fell off. His hands must have slipped. The grab bars were thick; his hands were, like mine, probably too small to get a tight grip. The scenario played itself over inside my head. I'd done that, ran after the coal truck, jumped on, felt hands slip, watched the spinning black wheels and in an instant fell clear. My stomach was sick inside.

The ambulance siren whined away, farther and farther, softer and softer. By the time it couldn't be heard it was pulling into the hospital grounds behind the spiked iron fence where nobody wanted to go. Somebody said the poor mother was gathered into somebody's car. She wouldn't ride in the police car and the ambulance wouldn't take her because she was hysterical.

The milling went on for a while, then dwindled as people in twos or threes, some holding their kids tighter than before, headed back to their houses, or stopped for a while, talking, visiting on some of the stoops. They only visited when there was an event, something unusual or disturbing. Other times they were hidden inside, doing the daily inside stuff. Outside was for kids.

Our band of kids stayed together that afternoon. We played close, quiet. The Carmody's wanted to play cops 'n robbers, a take on hide 'n seek. Their father was a cop. My sister pleaded for skaters to go around the block with her. No takers. There wasn't much play in us. Somebody asked if the kid was in heaven yet. Who knew?

The idea for the collection emerged. Nobody remembers who said it. Bobby Carmody got out the wagon he and his brother Jacky used to collect newspapers to take to the salvage yard on Saturday's. It was how we got movie money. We went with him collecting in the tenements. The old ladies mostly would give us their piled up papers and sometimes soda bottles or milk bottles that we traded at the store for the nickel deposit. We figured the wagon would hold a lot of stuff.

We went to the corner drug store first, because the druggist was always nice to us. I got put up front of the asking group, because I was the smallest and my blond hair made me harmless, and I was a girl. Jackie said that. The druggist gave us a bottle of aspirin for the Missus, because she'd need it with a dead kid, and a one pound box of chocolates.

Then we went to the Italian grocer. He knew most of us because our mothers all had bills with him. When money was tight or when you didn't get to Hoyle Square you could get most anything there, on the cuff, that's what they called credit. My father told me it was called that because in the old days the store owner would write the amount owed on his cuff. It must have been a strange looking cuff. I wondered when the old days were, but there was just so much I could ask my father before he got sick of my questions. The Italian gave us Scotch ham, thick slices of meat cut off an uncooked ham or shoulder, a poor man's ham dinner fried in a skillet; he gave a loaf of the cheapest bread, and two bags of canned goods. We went to the cleaners and the lady there gave us a dollar and gave each of us, we'd swelled to seven of us by then, lollipops from the Kiddies jar for being so kind.

So it went. Mr. Loving, who owned the house where I lived and owned the brown house, Early Arms where the kid lived, gave $2.00. Charley, his driver, gave fifty cents. We went to houses where we knew people, except for the Greeks. We were afraid of the Greeks but nobody knew why. They talked funny English and the old father didn't speak English at all. People gave bread or cookies or canned beans or soup or beer or apples, whatever they had. We filled the two boxes in the wagon to overflowing.

Mrs. O'Flannery, who was supposed to be a hundred and four, didn't give food or money. She wanted us to clean the papers and bottles out of her back entry. We said no. We'd do it Saturday. She gave us three milk bottles from the Red and White store where we got a nickel deposit each. Most of the time Red and White wouldn't give kids the deposit money. They wanted the purchaser to bring the bottles in. Probably thought we stole them, which we sometimes did. Jackie went into the Red and White store. I couldn't go in; I was banned from Red and White since I stole a candy bar. The grocer at Red and White gave Jackie the fifteen cents for the bottles and a whole bologna. I never knew anyone to get a whole bologna, thick and fat and greasy to the touch; he didn't wrap it, just gave it to Jackie whole.

Two boxes collected and nearly five dollars. Paul and Bobby, Judy, my sister Lois, and Earl and Sharky Elliot and me, we did it. Sharky Elliot wasn't sure we should give them all the money. Earl Elliot slugged his younger brother in the shoulder. It's what we expected. They were Protestants and they didn't have to go to confession on Saturday afternoon after the movies.

"You know the kid heard you in heaven," Earl said. Sharky looked skyward and waved his hand in front of his face as if he could wave away the thought before it reached the kid. I never knew till that day that Protestants knew about heaven.

We headed over to the brown house. It was getting dark. It was quiet. The light was on in the upstairs front where the kid's mother lived, alone now. We lifted the wagon onto the porch that ran across the front entryway between the two wings of the building. We rang the bell. We heard the footsteps coming down the stairs. A cold chill shivered through my body. My Grandmother told me when people died the Banshee was about and to stay away from the dead. A young girl answered the door, the kid's cousin she told us. She beckoned us in. We pulled the wagon into the hallway. Bobby wouldn't leave it on the porch. Between us, taking some things out of the boxes, we carried the stuff up two flights. The landings were dark, with only a bare bulb in what used to be an elegant entryway chandelier. It had an old and cold smell from not being heated. The girl opened the door at the top of the stairs and went through. We stood looking through the doorway. She waved us all in.

Father Dunn, the priest, was there. I saw him first, and then the kid's mother with a sweater across her shoulders, and then, on the sofa propped up with pillows and covers, was the kid! Not dead. Not in heaven. He wore a weak grin on his face and bandages on a head not a cracked open melon. There was chattering and thanking and Father Dunn, who normally frowned or whined at us, was saying soft things and patting our heads and shaking our shoulders and made the sign of the cross on all our foreheads, even Earl and Sharky who were protestants. The kid stared at us sheepishly.

"We thought you were killed," Sharky said, "so we collected this stuff cause the neighborhood thinks you're dead."

Sharky said out load the disappointment we all felt, Jesus, Mary and Joseph forgive us, and I silently crossed myself. We were doing good. Maybe we weren't heroes, but we were good guys. We weren't always, but on this one our hearts were pure. Now it was gone! The mission folded over us like too much mayonnaise on a white bread cheese sandwich.

The kid winced, as if to apologize for being alive.

"You did a good thing," Father Dunn answered, and told us the neighborhood would understand. We bundled our parcels onto the table and Jackie stuffed the five dollars and box of chocolates into the poor woman's hands and we headed for the door.

"You come and play," the kid's mother said. But I knew we wouldn't.

I don't remember much else. For a long while I stayed out of the way of the people we collected from and out of the drug store and the grocers. The next Saturday I went to Mrs. O'Flannery's and cleaned her back entry papers and swept the corners like she liked, better than I had ever done. I don't think any of us jumped on the coal truck again.

The First Rock

Things could get out of hand at Dick Loving's tenement house where my family lived. We were like a little community, but things didn't always go well for people there. Tony Marsucci lived on the third floor with his family. There were seven people stuffed into the three-room top floor front apartment where they lived. Dick Loving gave them an extra storage room for sleeping when the daughter got married and moved home; it was next to the bathroom they all shared with the three other single-room occupants.

Tony wanted to work for Dick Loving after he quit school in the 10th grade, be in his gang, he'd tell anyone who'd listen. Of course nobody called Loving's business a gang. He owned lots of property and a big diner out on Elmwood Avenue where some of the big gangsters in the city hung out. There was even a big shooting there once. Jenny's father was there when the cops raided the place; Dick Loving made him hide in the food storage room until the shooting and the raid stopped. It was before his night shift at the railroad, and he was late clocking in that night, and later still getting on the job because he had a story to tell. He used to go to the diner sometimes before work or after to play the numbers game, gambling for that big illusive someday prize that would change his family's lives. Of course, he mostly never won. Loving watched over him to see that he didn't lose too much and sometimes when he was at the diner he'd have the chef make chicken sandwiches to send to Jenny and the other kids and her mother. Loving had his ideas about the people who lived in his tenements. He was the patron, the overseer of his tenants, those he came to favor. Tony was one of those.

Dick Loving talked to Tony and told him at seventeen he'd better join the army and get away from Friendship Street and some of the bad apples he hung with in the neighborhood. It wasn't actually a big brotherly or fatherly sort of conversation. Tony took it as a command from the boss man, took the meaning of his word and enlisted. Dick Loving could see Tony was moving in a bad direction; the army would head that off. He didn't want a kid like Tony going bad on his watch. He went with Tony to talk with Mrs. Marsucci, his mother, to convince her to sign the papers for Tony to enlist.

Tony's mother cried and cried, wiping her face with the flowered apron she always wore. Dick Loving told her it was best, and his word was law. She didn't want her family to be evicted from the tenement. She knew if Tony went bad Loving would throw the whole family out. He didn't want bad people in his places.

Tony's sister Roseanna planned a big going away party. With Dick Loving's okay she and friends set up a couple of card tables in the driveway beside the tenement house. They hung crepe paper in red white and blue and a hand printed cardboard sign that read "Bon Voyage Tony." They all got drunk, except the neighborhood kids who got Royal Cola or Orange soda. Jenny and her sister Lois and even her little brother were there to celebrate Tony. Jenny knew there wasn't much to celebrate on Friendship Street. That's what she told her mother when she asked if they could go to the party while she was at work. She promised to take care of her brothers.

Everyone in the tenement and Tony's friends were coming. Jenny's mother gave her a dollar to give to Tony for his going away.

Somebody called Dick Loving when the party got out of hand and the cops showed up. It was probably old man Elliot who called the cops. He owned the big house next door. His wife and kids lived on the first floor, all of it. The top two floors were taken up by boarders. Mrs. Elliot cooked breakfast and dinner for them. A real old fashioned boarding house, mostly sick old ladies and reformed drunks. They all liked quiet, and Tony Marsucci's party was too noisy for them.

Three cops showed up, two cars. They got out, night sticks swinging side by side so nobody could miss the action. Break up the party, the cops told them. Jenny gave her little brother to her sister Lois and sent the ten year old into the house. For a while she stood in the side doorway that lead to their basement apartment.

Things were going okay when the cop in charge suddenly decided Tony was too drunk to leave on the street and had to go downtown. They were going to take him in, and everyone knew what Tony knew. If he went to jail, he'd miss the early morning bus and the swearing in at the old port. He wouldn't get to join the army. Tony tried to talk to them, convince them he'd go home, upstairs. The party would be over. The cop in charge was adamant. Downtown. He gestured to the squad car and Tony got in the back seat.

Nobody saw the first rock fly. Later there was talk of who did it. The barrage followed. There were kids on the garage roof, all young teens, Jenny with them, throwing rocks. The cops shouted for them to get down. They scattered. The fat cop decided to run after them. The kids skipped off the back of the roof. The Carmody kids, whose dad was a cop ran around the corner and into their house to watch out the second floor window. Others skipped across the fence and dashed home. Jenny and Jackie and a couple of other boys headed into the three story apartment house across the lot. The fat cop chased them. Jenny ran up to the fourth floor and up the fire escape ladder and wedged herself, feet and shoulder, against the glass skylight that was locked. She could hear the fat cop puffing up the stairs, swearing under his breath. She stayed still, pushing hard on her feet and shoulders to keep from falling. She heard him stop at the top of the stairway. She could imagine him staring down the long corridor. She prayed to herself to ask Holy Mary to keep the tenants from opening their doors. She heard the cop's last expletive as he turned and banged his way down the stairs. Jenny stayed quiet, wedged in the skylight for a long time.

Two cops came back to the party after a while, three kids in tow. One, the girl, got away. The blond kid, the little one.

She's the worst somebody told the cops. She's just twelve somebody else called from the group. They wanted to know where she lived. The group was silent. The unwritten rule, nobody told cops anything. They knew, those that were up on the roof, she'd thrown the first rock. The cops whacked the kids on their heads and yelled for them to get home. Jenny sneaked across Carmody's backyard and climbed back up on the roof, laying flat so she could watch what was happening. She prayed to the Holy Mother to save Tony so he could go to the army.

Tony was in the back of the squad car looking pretty forlorn. His mother pleaded. It was just a going away party. Everyone wanted to wish Tony good luck. He was lucky getting out of the neighborhood. It was what Mr. Loving wanted. Tears streamed down her face. She knew, everyone knew, the cops knew that Tony was not going to get his dream.

The long black Caddy drove up across the driveway, blocking the cop car that had angled onto the party scene. The driver got out, and the man beside him, a heavy set man who looked like a boxer got out. He went around and opened the back door. Dick Loving pushed himself out and walked to the cop car where Tony was peering through the closed window. He was shaking his head, almost sadly it seemed. Jenny watched from her roof perch and breathed a sigh of relief. Dick Loving would save Tony.

"Carmody," he said, beckoning the lead cop to him, rolling his pointer finger. "What's this?"

Carmody was a large round man, maybe just short of six feet. His belly rounded over the belt that held his baggy pants just beneath it. His thick neck supported a thicker head upon which sat the hat of distinction in this neighborhood. Cop. All cop. Feared by most of the neighbors when he showed up. He had power to change lives, to drag kids or grownups downtown and into the less than justice system.

Here was Tony, about to feel the clamping of the law on his

dreams. Just too much to drink. party gone sour. That's what Carmody said. Dick Loving looked around. He saw Tony's mother sobbing. She was the one who paid the rent for the seven people who she squeezed into the upstairs apartment and room. She was the one who made their excuses, who nursed them when they were sick or drunk. Loving was glad for her when he heard Tony was going into the army. There was pride in that, he told her, the first she'd known with any of her family. There were a few quiet words exchanged, mostly Dick Loving whispering in the side of Carmody's face.

Carmody nodded his head, shook it firmly, put his hands in his pants pockets shaking the loose change he had there. The cuffs dangled on his belt. His gun was slid a little behind and below the belt. Loving gestured to the side with his head toward the car door to the boxer beside him; he pointed his chin, and with his eyes the message was clear. Get the door of the police car door.

The boxer opened the door. Tony climbed out. He grabbed Dick Loving and clung to him, life restored, the vision revived.

"Let'm go," Carmody said.

The smallish blond girl now stood by the side door in the alley that opened to the two room basement apartment where she lived with her mother and father and three more kids. She could see everything. Loving watched her for a minute, then he walked over to her. He put his hands on the sides of her head, covering her ears, and shook her head.

"This is not for you," he said. "You go inside and do your homework, study your school work."

She looked at Dick Loving, into the shining dark eyes that smiled at her.

" I did it," she whispered, "threw the first rock." She knew he was good to her mother, to her family. He wouldn't tell, but she wanted him to know, to be honest with him.

"This is not for you," he said again. He softly patted the side of her face with his hand, like a slap but not. "No rocks, no fighting, no bad behavior. You are different. Go inside."

The message was understood. She was under his protection. She was not a part of all of this. He could save this one, he could save her. He could save Tony.

"Party's over." Dick loving said so. The cops got into the squad cars and drove away. They wouldn't be back that night.

The next morning Dick Loving showed up at six thirty to drive Tony and his mother to the swearing in ceremony. He went inside and watched Tony raise his hand and promise loyalty. It was loyalty to the government, and to the army. Both Tony and Dick knew there was another loyalty. When he came home, when the army was done with him Dick Loving would be waiting and Tony would remain loyal to him. After the ceremony Tony was whisked off to the airport to fly to his boot camp. Dick Loving drove Tony's mother home, gave her twenty dollars, promising her he'd be okay. If Dick could help it he would be.

Later in the morning a few neighbors cleaned up the mess from the party, took down the crepe paper ribbons and the sign. The blond girl missed school that day. She slept too late. She walked outside and watched the women cleaning up. She went over to the dip where the driveway connected to the street and picked up two rocks. Maybe they were the rocks she'd thrown. She slipped them into her pocket and took them inside. Years later they sat on the wide desk in her office at the university where she was Professor of American Studies. She never forgot Tony's party.

Tony didn't come home to pay allegiance to the Boss of the neighborhood. He was killed in Vietnam some ten years later. Most people forgot about him. His mother remembered and Jenny grown woman remembered. Loving saved Tony so he could die a hero. The lesson was lost on her.

The Summer Party

Dick Loving was a simple man with simple dreams. He had a business, not the best in the world, but one that paid him well. He ran numbers, a gambling scheme, and women, and loans and things like that. He kept order in his business like people in his business did. He wasn't always nice but he did what he had to do. He had a real estate business. He owned houses; he was a slum lord some said, but he knew he did good for the people who lived in his houses and paid rent on time. Once in a while when they didn't he carried them along, of course with an extra consideration.

Every summer he gave a party for the people in his houses. He thought the mix of people was good, the people from the nicer Silver Lake and the west side areas, and some of the upper class tenants from around Washington Park, and his favorites, from Friendship Street. He had four places around Friendship Street, all reconditioned mansions that he turned into small apartments. He was generous. He let families with kids move in. It was just after the war and flats and apartments were scarce. Take the biggest place on Friendship Street: two three room apartments on the first two floors; two two-room places on the third floor and four single room efficiency apartments; and the basement, two rooms, kitchen and bath and the use of the cellar for laundry and playroom for the kids.

Jenny's family that lived there in the two rooms; there were four kids; they were good kids and their parents were good hard working people, except the father was a drunk and gambled at Dick Loving's places. He was into Dick for a good bit of money. Dick Loving tried to get Jenny's mother and father to let him adopt their baby boy. He was a chubby dark eyed boy; he could pass for Armenian. That's the French in him Jenny's father said when he'd talked with them about it. Jenny learned the story from her mother later, after it was clear the baby wasn't going to be taken away. Loving and Ginger needed a baby. She couldn't have kids, and they couldn't pass the adoption screening. In Jenny's family there were four kids. What was one more or less? Her mother wouldn't hear of it though; in fact, she'd told Dick Loving it was the worst thing she'd ever heard. She'd never give up her kid. They were good parents, good and stupid. Dick Loving thought they were selfish. The kid would grow up poor; maybe get a trade. He and Ginger could send him to college, give him everything, money no object. In fact, at the last offer he suggested money. He knew that was illegal. A simple private adoption would be okay. His lawyer said not to mention money. Ginger was desperate; he gave them a number. They turned it down flat. It wasn't about money. But Dick Loving told them the money could help them move out of the neighborhood, give the other kids a good life as well.

They'd come to the summer party, they said. Maybe, Dick thought, if they saw his place and all he could give the boy, maybe they'd change their minds.

Charley Long Nose was the driver who picked some of the people from Friendship Street up at the corner in front of the house. He used the big limo and with squeezing, there were ten people, mostly kids. The grownups would come in the next car. All in all three cars came to pick up 22 people at Friendship Street, and two people drove themselves.

Jenny didn't know then that Dick and Ginger Loving asked to adopt her baby brother, not until Ginger told her at the party. She thought maybe kid would think it was a good idea. Ginger was showing her around the house; it was a big three story house, all for one family. Dick's mother lived in the first floor front apartment and he had his offices in the back. The top two floors were for Dick and Ginger, just the two of them, and about six bird cages with canaries and a couple of parrot like birds. They were Ginger's birds. She couldn't have kids. Later Jenny remembered telling her that was too bad.

The party was in the back yard. It was like four back yards, surrounded by a ten foot high chain link fence. In the back was a section for four German shepherd dogs, watch dogs, somebody said. All around the fence were high hedges and just inside them raised bushes, flowering shrubs, lilacs. Then there were flower beds, better than at the park, all designed by Ginger, but the work was done by a gardener, she laughed as she told a group of woman standing in a clutch. She held out her long bright red manicured fingernails. The ladies oohed and ahhed. Some unconsciously pushed their own work wearied hands into pockets or behind backs. They didn't garden either. Their gardens were jewelry factories where they punched out or packaged or worked findings on gold and silver filigreed flowers.

The food smells were incredible. Whoever ate shish kabob before? What is it, people asked, or others, wanting to be more sophisticated remembered having it the year before, at the last year's party. Yummy. Good. Lamb, fruit, tomatoes, onions, peppers, spices. Jenny waited on the hot dog line. That suited her. American food. She didn't like Chinese and was sure she wouldn't like Armenian. The best of all was desert. Ginger asked Jenny to go upstairs with her to help her carry down the plates of cakes and cookies. She looked over the table covered with a wide assortment of desserts. She had not seen so much delicious looking fare, especially the high pink frosted angel food cake, beautiful to look at, a shame to cut, and later a sweet treat that just melted in the mouth. Jenny had three pieces, sneaking the extras after most people had eaten. Ginger wanted her to know about Dick's family. They were brave. He was born in America, but his mother and her brothers escaped from the old country. The boys were at risk of being caught and maybe even killed, she told Jenny. The mothers cut the long hair from the girls, and using scarves tied it onto the boys' heads, dressed them like girls and smuggled them onto the ships to escape. It was a heroic story. When Jenny saw the ancient Armenian mother who was the root of this family she was awed, yet held back from taking the long withered hand she held out.

Ginger spoke Armenian to her. Jenny didn't understand it; the language sounds were uncomfortable to me. Ginger told me her told the Mother-in-law Jenny was the sister of the boy who would be hers one day soon. Jenny stared at her shocked, then quickly pulled away to go and find her mother. She saw her out in the backyard sitting on a wooden garden chair plumped with pillows. She held the baby brother in her lap.

"I want to go home," Jenny told her.

"No," her mother answered, "it's too early. The cars won't return until seven o'clock. Beside I'm having a good time."

Jenny picked her little brother up and carried him across the yard. Her mother was always relieved when somebody took him from her. He was her late child. The next youngest was ten years older, and she was embarrassed to have a baby at her age. Jenny remembered how often she told her that. Jenny had her brother's diaper bag and bottles. She found a patch of grass shaded and protected by some bushes and hid out there. He curled over with his bottle and was soon sleeping.

Ginger and her mother came over to see him.

"Let me hold him," Ginger said.

"No," Jenny whispered, getting up and positioning herself between Ginger and the baby, "he's asleep."

"You see," Jenny's mother laughed at her. "Even if I wanted to, she'd never let me give him away."

Somewhere in the root of her being was a sense of horror. It spun down and down and caused great trembling in her soul.

Ginger laughed, no doubt seeing the horror frozen on Jenny's face. "I bet she'd give in for that great TV we have," she said.

"Did you see that TV?" Jenny's mother asked her.

No. Jenny shook her head furiously feeling nearly convulsing. "You don't trade babies for TV's! Jenny remembered their laughing at her. Ginger told her she was a silly girl. Maybe she should get more cake. She and Jenny's mother were going to take care of the baby. No, she told them. She'd watch him, lie down and rest with him. They went away.

She watched them seemingly bound together talking as they sat and sipped drinks. Her mother looked like she belonged in this beautiful place. It was one of her dreams, to have a beautiful home. The dream was far away from the cellar apartment on Friendship Street. Jenny always loved her dream, but on that day, with all the glitter and good food and seeming friendship surrounding her she became somebody Jenny didn't know.

While her mother and Ginger were talking, Jenny gathered up the baby and his satchel and made for the side gate out of the garden and headed down the street. She carried the baby down the street for a while and then cut across a couple of back alleys to get as far away from Dick Loving's house as fast as she could. She didn't know where she was. With the few coins in her pocket she bought an apple pie and a coke in a grocery store. The baby still had milk. He liked the pie and Jenny fed most of it to him. He was heavy as she walked. She was not sure how far it was home. It was getting dark. She imagined it was later than eight o'clock. She sat in a doorway along the route resting before going on. At some point along the way she recognized the neighborhood; she was above her Nana's neighborhood. It was refuge; it was a safe place. She'd help save her little brother. She wouldn't let them give him away. It was dark as she started down Pavilion Avenue. Lights were on in all the houses. People could be seen sitting in living rooms or around dining room tables. Not like Friendship Street, there was warmth here. These were not strangers. Just beyond the top of the hill she could see Nana's house. There were strange cars out front. She sat on the porch of Mrs. Gagan's place. She was old and always kept to the bedroom in the back of the house. Jenny rocked the baby. He was restless and whiney. She was out of milk for him and the pie was gone. He probably needed his diaper changed. She waited a while before she saw people come out of the house and get into the cars. Nana came along with them and after waving goodbye went back into her house. Quietly Jenny carried the baby down the hill, went to the side door and slipped inside. Nana never kept the door locked. One never knew when family would be stopping by. The radio was playing and Jenny could hear Nana in the kitchen singing one of her hymns, just beyond the hallway door. She sang hymns when she was worried. It was like praying but easier. Jenny began to sob; then the baby started to cry.

The door opened. "Jesus, Mary and Joseph," Nana shouted, making the sign of the cross, head, heart, across her shoulders and kissed her hand as ever, "there you are." She came and took Jenny into her arms, Jenny and the baby. She led her into the kitchen, then beyond into the front room.

"We thought you were kidnapped. The police...." she left off. Jenny thought the police would be coming for her as soon as the words left her mouth. Nana just held on to Jenny as she rambled through the story of the party and the baby being given away.

"Wouldn't be the worst thing for the poor baby," she said. n a heartbeat she repeated that wistful dream that imagined rescue from poverty and pain. Maybe there was rescue. It was the thought immediately repressed, pushed away from the horror of loss.

"They can't have the baby," Jenny said.

" That's what your mother told them. She said you'd never let the baby go. She wouldn't either," Nana added.

So after, when they cried and talked and laughed about Jenny's great rescue adventure, the story of how the boy almost became the heir to a great fortune, it was always told that Jenny was the one who said no. Even today she isn't sure they did the right thing. The baby brother grew up not exactly poor, but no heir to a fortune. He made his own, in his own way, with his family and his work. He became a craftsman, earned a good living and loved his life. Jenny often wondered if he ever heard the story of his near rescue from wealth. The other part of the story Jenny never told anyone was the thought she had following Ginger through the lovely big home seeing the wealth and comfort and the gaping need she had to love a child, the plea that begged silently in Jenny's heart,

"Why don't you take me?"

But then, who would have taken care of the baby?

They Didn't Let Chappie Join the Army
... a long story

Chappie wasn't always a drinker. He was one of the casualties of the Second World War. Not in the usual sense. His brother Frank was in the Coast Guard; he rose high in the ranks so his office was in Washington, D.C. and didn't have the fear of harm that some felt. His brother Edmund was too old for the draft; he was a trainman, a conductor on the New Haven Railroad. Fr. Arthur, the oldest brother, was a priest somewhere in Belgium trying to carry on the Lord's work in face of a brutal war. It made his mother worry; she prayed a lot, especially for Fr. Arthur, who, she said, needed her prayers most.

Chappie didn't get drafted. He tried to enlist but was refused. He was told the trains were vital. He told the draft board somebody else could stay in his place. He was refused.

"I shoud'a gone," he told Edmund.

"Well, the rails are essential service, so they won't let you join," Edmund responded. "You ought to be glad to stay home. What good of it if you got killed and Annie got left alone with the three kids?"

Edmund could never remember Chappie's kids' names. He didn't much care whether they'd be okay or not. He cared that Chappie got a deferment. His mother didn't need to worry about her youngest going off to war. Edmund thought the war was a waste. If he'd been better informed about the political conditions in the country he might have been an isolationist. It didn't matter to him. What mattered was the family was safe and hung together.

Chappie went to Frank in the Coast Guard to see if he could get the deferment removed. Frank talked about it with Edmund. They both agreed it was too much to ask, the baby of the family going off to war, just after their father died from a bad appendix and worse medical care.

Chappie did what many young able men did when denied the war. He avoided places where the troops were when they were on furlough, or where the Navy guys were when they came back to town from Newport or Quonset Point. They wore their uniforms, had to. Chappie found himself hiding out, not wanting to go anywhere, not wanting to be named a draft dodger.

"Take the kids to the park," Annie said.

"No."

"Take them to the movies."

"No."

"Come to church."

"No."

It was a continual procession of no's to all of her requests. He wouldn't help her shop. He wouldn't even visit her mother's house for Sunday dinner. He was an outcast; he made himself a pariah. They talked about it. Annie talked with Edmund and to Frank when he was home. She talked with their wives and with some of her women friends who brought their babies to the play park. She went to work at the shipyard.

"My own little Rosie the Riveter," Chappie said when she came home after her first day on the job.

"I'm just doing the sorting after the other people do their jobs and sometimes assemble things."

She had a job from three to eleven. That way between her mother and Chappie the kids didn't have to go to day care. Still, she smiled when Chappie chucked her under the chin and gave her a kiss on her forehead.

It's hard to pinpoint when Chappie started drinking. It was slow, unnoticed, mostly after Annie was at work and the kids went to bed. Annie didn't get home, what with overtime and all, until sometimes one in the morning. He was asleep by then. She noticed he'd taken to chewing on Sen Sen, a kind of breath freshener. She didn't think why he'd do that. She didn't like the scent of him. Lots of time she'd lie down on the parlor couch and pull a coverlet over her and sleep.

Other people noticed before Annie did. Her mother mentioned that he seemed odd lately.

"Well, it was understandable, being at home, and able bodied and all," her mother said.

"He couldn't enlist; he tried; he tried and tried." Annie defended Chappie.

They moved to Friendship Street before the war ended. It was Chappie's idea. He wanted to move away from the family stomping grounds, from the Irish mothers whose sons were off in the war, from Mrs. Cote, who had a gold star in her window, dead sons lost in the Pacific. He wanted to be where nobody knew him. That didn't suit Annie, but who was she to fight back, even though it was harder to get to her job at the shipyard. From Pavilion Avenue she walked down the avenue, cross a main street and wandered down the dead end dirt road to the beach, cross the sand to the factory where she worked on assembling some of the parts used in building the boats. Since moving to Friendship Street she had to take two buses.

"Well, I don't like it one bit," her mother said. Like Annie she didn't complain to Chappie. He was the man of the house. He was the law of the family. Never mind the kids could no longer run to Nana's house if they needed her. Never mind the house up the hill from the family home was a cheap rental, and the place on Friendship Street cost a little more. It did have more rooms, a parlor, a kitchen and a dining room and four bedrooms. It was one of the big old houses that used to be classy before the city shifted and the rich people left the big houses to the Irish and the Italians.

It was a big Victorian that used to be one family, three floors for one family. The top floor was not so decorated Annie noticed. The first floor flat had decorative wood, fancy carving and mahogany trim. The second floor had cherry wood, not so fancy; it was where the family bedrooms used to be. The second floor was split into two apartments, four rooms each with a shared bathroom between them. The top floor was had just a little trim, plain wood, for the servants Annie's mother said. Annie didn't know, but it seemed maybe she was right. It was split into two apartments with a shared bath, not as big as the second floor bath, but still shared by two families, and four single rooms rented to single people.

Annie didn't want to admit she liked the flat. It was prettier and had more room than their Pavilion Avenue rental.

"More to heat," Annie told her mother. "It's pretty enough, though."

"More work to keep up," her mother responded. She wouldn't ever like it. It took her daughter away from her. When she did condescend to visit she had to take the trolley almost to downtown.

Fewer prying eyes, Chappie thought to himself. On Friendship Street they didn't know people like they did on Pavilion Avenue, where the families were already second generation Irish. Most of them came from County Monaghan in Ireland, some on the same boat they used to laugh. Chappie was the only son who didn't go off to war except Harry Clements who was an epileptic; he could hardly leave the house never mind enlist in the service.

On Friendship Street Chappie didn't have to hide out so much. He went to the corner drug store and bought beer and whiskey. The grocery store was not too bad. The grocer had black market chicken and a few other things once in a while for a price, not that the family needed much or took advantage of it often.

Toward the end of the war Chappie gave up his car. Gas was hard to come by anyway. The more he drank, the less money he had for necessities like car expenses. Annie made good money, but she was putting some of it aside for the day they could buy a house. Someday, after the war, they'd buy a house. It was Annie' dream.

The end of the war came. There were celebrations. The radio was on all day so Annie could hear the latest news. When she and the kids went to her mother's for Sunday dinner, Chappie never went now, the end of the war and what it meant was all the talk. Guys wore their uniforms after the fighting stopped. The Gold Star Mothers, more of them now, kept their star flags in the windows. At the local bars there was big talk about the battles, the ships, the European war, and the Pacific campaigns. Chappie listened quietly, and if asked to tell about his experiences, he just faded back, smiling. Nobody wanted to hear about his riding trains down to the Navy yard, or about the night half a train loaded with ammunition blew up. He was brakeman on that train; he knew almost all of the twelve guys who got killed, the ones on the train and the ones at the station where the train was slowing to a stop. It looked like a war zone they saw in the newsreels at the movies. He wasn't sure why he survived himself.

It was a brave thing to make up those trains, handle cars stuffed with guns and ammo and dangerous things. He knew that. The guys he worked with knew that. A few of them were held back from the army but for the most part they were older guys, too old for the draft. Nobody sick got to work for the railroad. It was too dangerous, hard work.

"Whadaya think, Chappie?" somebody asked. By that time, Chappie was a habitual drunk. Nobody paid much attention to him. Chappie shrugged off conversation and buried himself in his beer. After the war he bid on a dayshift job, seven to four. Most nights after work he stopped at the bar; he stayed until it closed at ten. He was in no hurry to go home and find Annie up. She was asleep when he came home or pretended she was. In the early morning he got up and dressed and went to work before she and the kids got up.

If anyone told Annie Chappie was a drunk she'd deny it or turn away. Not her Chappie. Annie hoped for more in her life. She and Chappie had dreams once. There was an imagined little house at the edge of the country. There were better schools for the kids, and maybe a new car. Lately, Annie thought about how she might get her husband back. This was after a bout of several months when she wanted desperately to have him leave, disappear. She didn't say divorce. That was forbidden. She met with Father Finnegan several times. He told her Chappie was her cross to bear. He gave her the name of a doctor who he thought might be able to help Chappie, and if not, at least help her manage her life, cope, he said. She'd never heard that word before. The priest told her that her husband had an illness. She had to stay and support him. Such was the thinking in Annie's life and from those around her.

Annie made an appointment for Chappie and her to see the doctor. The visit turned into three visits. The doctor gave Chappie medicine that would make him sick if he drank. That was one way to avoid the devil drink. The doctor talked with Annie about how she was partly responsible for Chappie's drinking and she had to stop putting demands on him he couldn't meet. Annie didn't know she did that. She tried to recall what demands she placed on him. None came to mind.

After a few bouts of severe stomach pain and throwing up Chappie gave up the medicine and gave up the doctor. Annie went to the last visit, which was like no visit because without Chappie there the doctor said there was nothing to talk about. When she left she felt she'd been abandoned, by the doctor, by her church, by her husband. There was nowhere to turn. She wished she could find solace as Chappie did, in the drink. That never worked for her. It just gave her a serious headache. And she had kids to take care of. Life on Friendship Street went on, day after day. It was okay, manageable for her and the kids. Chappie, most of the time, brought home his paycheck. She knew of some men who didn't. At least she had that comfort.

It was her mother who brought the news that her sister Marilyn was going to buy a house with her husband Benny. They had the new GI bill benefits, a nice little house for no money down and low payments. Also, Benny was going to go to college with all the bills paid and he's even get a paycheck for going, some payback for being in the army for two years. Too bad Chappie didn't get to go to the army. Annie knew Benny spent the war years in San Diego. He was a clerk in an office and never got inside a ship or near a gun. He was probably in less danger than Chappie riding on the back of the ammo trains in all kinds of weather, freezing cold or boiling hot. Annie wanted to be happy for Marilyn and Benny. She tried hard to smile when her mother sipped her tea across the table, her face joyful at this happy family news.

"It's sure nice somebody in the family is a success."

Annie turned her face away, looking out across the grassless backyard of the house that had become a parking lot for the people in the tenement house. Tears welled up behind her eyelids; she fought to hold them back. Her mother's words cut into her. During the war she had worked so hard. Chappie had worked hard on the trains. He wanted to be in the army or the Coast Guard or anywhere anyone would take him. It didn't seem fair. He was classified as a special needs worker and had to stay on the trains.

There were no words to say to her mother. She knew her mother was angry with Chappie for moving his family to Friendship Street. It was, after all, not the best of neighborhoods. The kids were okay, not running with the wildest bunch. They were good students. They weren't in the Catholic school any more. There wasn't enough money for tuition or books, and the kids liked the public junior high school better. During the war they all saved scrap for the war drives and bought war bonds and the kids got stamps at school and helped fill and pack boxes for the starving kids in Europe. Annie didn't know how she'd tell the kids about Aunt Marilyn's and Uncle Benny's new house. She didn't know how to answer them in earlier years when they asked why their Daddy didn't have to go to war. She explained Chappie had a really important job, making sure the trains carried the supplies and ammunition needed for the war effort. She knew they, like Chappie and like herself, had to answer the questions or the taunts that the outside world laid on them. They had to reassure themselves, all of them, that Chappie was brave in his own way. He had no choice. The government didn't let him go to war.

Chappie took the news of the new house in his stride. It was good for them, he said. They deserved it. After all, Benny might have been killed.

"Not in the office in San Diego," she answered almost bitterly, as if, she thought, she almost wished it on him.

"He could have been disabled, wounded in the war' they could've sent him overseas anytime," Chappie said. He liked Benny; he worried about him when he was posted across the country.

"You were disabled," Annie said, "you became a drunk because of all of this."

The talking stopped. He stared at her for a long time, until having enough, she turned and raced into the kitchen from the living room where they were sitting. Funny things happened after that. Annie thought, but might have been wrong, that Chappie was drinking less.

"He's hiding it better," her mother said. He didn't give her any more money, sometimes less. But it was regular. He didn't disappear for a day or two at a time at the end of the week like he used to do. They didn't talk about it. He came home earlier at night, but still stopped at the bar.

They went out to visit the now famous new house; it took almost a year to get the houses in the plat where Benny and Marilyn were buying the tiny two bedroom one bath they'd chosen. It was a great day. The whole neighborhood was invited. Not only were Benny and Marilyn moving, but four other couples from the neighborhood, all friends from high school who went off to war together also bought houses in the same plat. It was almost like the old avenue where the families moved in from Ireland. They'd have a shared history, they'd be friends for life. The party was jammed, moving from one half furnished house to another, lifting a glass or passing chips and pretzels around while the kids ran in and out, bringing in muddy feet on the new carpets and listening to the grownups yelling about it, and Marilyn went in and out of rooms with a damp towel trying to spot clean the mud trails.

They were little houses. After the party quieted down, Chappie and Annie sat in Benny's and Marilyn's little living room. It had a real fireplace.

"We probably won't use it," Marilyn said, "so it won't get dirty."

"She's afraid to burn the house down," Benny laughed. Looking out the window the front lawn was all mud, but Benny said he had plans for new grass when spring came, and even some fencing around the lot. It was going to be an experiment for them, kind of like moving the old neighborhood families out to the suburbs. They'd all learn together. All the war veterans were going to begin a new pathway. Chappie had been one of them in high school. Not now though. Now he was an outsider, like he'd been throughout the war. America was rebuilding; America was on the move. Just some of the Americans who'd held the home front together were not joining in.

There wasn't much joining in with Benny and Marilyn after the party. Annie and the kids stopped going to Sunday dinner, since it was more often at Benny's and Marilyn's home, not at Nana's on Pavilion Avenue. They didn't have a dining room, and there wasn't space around the kitchen table for the whole extended family, even if the table was outside at a cookout.

Friendship Street took on a new look for Annie. The house, though older, was so much bigger than the suburban houses. Four bedrooms meant the three kids could all have a room of their own. And the big dining room had a long table, enough for the whole family. Annie didn't invite them these days. She invited, rather, some of the neighbors and their kids for holidays. Things went along. When her mother came to visit, she might comment on Annie's new sofa, or some fresh new curtains Annie made for the windows. Of course, they'd be compared to the beautiful Priscilla drapes, fluffy and sheer in Marilyn's living room, with a drum table and lamp right in the center of the picture window. Annie had a quick vision of the drum table in the picture window of every single house on the street where Benny and Marilyn lived. She mentioned it to her mother.

"Yes, well, you have to keep up."

Annie and Chappie had a momentum to their lives. Chappie still kept a full stock of drinks. Annie didn't notice the supply was more stable than it used to be. Some of the bottles got a little dusty. They didn't talk about it. Annie got a job at the new community center built down the street about four blocks from Friendship Street. She was the new community assistant and helped scheduled the many events that were beginning to happen. After the war there was redevelopment money for some of the older neighborhoods to help prevent crime: it was called Community improvement money. Annie worried about some of the families in the neighborhood, and she was able to help with food drives or special classes, and she helped get the neighbors together to insist upon a new swimming pool.

The kids were doing okay. Their older boy went to high school. He was a good student and enrolled in the Classical High School rather than the neighborhood high. He was going to college. Annie would see to it. Maybe even the girls would go.

"If he takes long enough, Benny might be in college at the same time," Chappie laughed. While not begrudging his brother-in-law his opportunity, Benny's dreams of a college education and fancy job on one of the newspapers in town were taking longer than planned. Marilyn had two more kids, and the money was needed to keep things going, including adding a room on the house. Benny was pulled between college classes and working a job to make ends meet.

Annie wasn't sad that Chappie didn't go away to war. She knew too many families that lost the men in their lives, too many families whose sons or husbands or fathers came home with serious physical or mental disabilities. She did get tired of people asking why her husband wasn't drafted, though she got used to it. She told her story of how he was in a special job, driving the ammo trains, more dangerous, she told people, than being in the war. She didn't believe that really. She had him close. That's all that mattered.
It was hard to think about the nice life out in the suburbs. They looked at a couple of houses and thought they might be able to buy. The houses were small, and the price was high, and without the GI

Bill the interest made the payments much more than the Friendship Street flat they rented.

Annie hated the way Marilyn said sub urbs, turning it into two words. She said she felt sorry for people left in the urbs, like Annie and Chappie. Annie thought she saw a smile on Marilyn's face when she heard the worst, that Chappie and Marilyn weren't going to be able to buy a place in the suburbs. A comedown her mother told Annie, but never mind. You'll get back up again.

The sadness didn't come all of a sudden on Annie. It came slowly, grain by grain, drip by drip as she saw the kids getting older and Chappie still drinking. She held it all together as best she could. She used to pray a lot until she gave it up. There didn't seem to be any point. Nothing mattered. She gave up caring whether the curtains were shabby, which they got to be after a few years in the flat. The curtains got limp and lost the brightness they had when she first sewed them and hung them. She was happy then, sure she'd make a home for them, however hard it seemed.

Her mother came now and again, fewer times as the years passed. Not much point in visiting Annie. It was pretty depressing. They were a family in trouble. Nobody noticed, not even the priest who came by on his twice yearly calls. He saw what wanted to see, not the realities of a difficult life brought on by the conditions around them. They were drowning, and there was no life ring to toss. Just pray he told Annie. The priest didn't see Chappie on his house calls. Chappie had no tolerance priests. Theirs was a different world. He was back on the night shift, so he slept most of the day.

The priest wasn't around the day Chappie found the small brown leather pouch in the gutter when he was walking home from work that morning. It was just after six. The shift got out early; the trains were all made up, the yard was clear. The foreman told the men to go home. It had been a rough week, cold and wet; they were all tired. Chappie walked up the avenue toward home. He wandered into the gutter where the sidewalk was all broken and uneven. His boot kicked a small pile of sodden leaves. He noticed a dark wet brown object roll out of the leaves. At first he was just going to walk on. Something made him look again. He reached down and picked it up. The zipper was encrusted with mud, and the bag itself, about eight inches square was sodden, sewn of soft leather. Chappie tried the zipper, but it didn't budge. It looked like a homemade tobacco pouch; there might be something in it he could salvage. He stuffed it in his jacket pocket; he'd work on it later.

Keenan's Bar was just ahead; he thought about getting his usual after work beer. Something made him turn away. He didn't remember turning away before. He was as regular as clock work, Keenan's after work. It was earlier than usual though. He decided to just go home. The kids wouldn't be up yet. Maybe he could slip in beside Annie for a warm snuggle. He liked it when she stirred from her sleep all bed warm, and he could wrap around her. It had been a long while. Usually she was up when he got home.

He entered the house quietly, crossed the kitchen area and went into the bedroom. The littlest boy, nearly two now, was sleeping soundly in his crib in the corner, and Annie was motionless, sprawled across a pillow, wrapped in the blanket she'd quilted years ago. He looked at her auburn hair sprinkled a little with gray. Tears filled his eyes. He'd disappointed her. She wanted more. Why did he think about that now? She stirred in her sleep, then turned over and opened her eyes looking up at him. He sat on the edge of the bed. He leaned across and took her in his arms. What was it about that moment? Why, when he wanted just to warm to her, he felt he had to hold back. He was unworthy. He was unworthy. She folded her arms around him. It was as if eons of time stripped away and they were, for just a few flashing moments entwined hearts that loved each other once.

The boy stirred in its crib, then the stir became a bellow and Chappie knew the moment was gone. She moved away, straightened the flannel nightgown around herself, and slipped out of bed. She was gone to him once again. He took off his clothes and slid beneath the still warm blanket, smelling the scent of her on the pillow he punched up under his head. He was almost sleeping when he heard her come back, a steaming cup of coffee for him. She hadn't done that in a while, a long while. He edged himself up and took the hot cup and savored it as she went about the morning tasks of getting the kids up and off to school.

It was a strange morning. She decided to dress and walk the children to school. She almost never did that. But this morning was like no other. He agreed to keep the boy with him until she returned. She dumped the two year old onto the bed, and Chappie gave him a hug and tussled a bit with him. Then, though tired after the cold night's work, he got up to make the boy breakfast.

The baby was in his high chair chewing on toast when Chappie remembered the bag. He went to the jacket he'd draped across the end of the bed and tugged the leather bag out of his pocket. He went into the bathroom and got a facecloth and wetted it, using it to clear the mud from the zipper. He tugged on it and eventually it opened. Inside the bag was a wad of money, damp, but intact, a lot of money. Also, wrapped in a piece of blue cloth he found two medals, war medals from the look of them, wrapped in a soiled ribbon. There was a necklace with a blue jewel wrapped in a thin letter. There was a small card, and he could barely read the name; it looked like Zimmerman. Some foreign writing he couldn't make out. The first name was illegible, faded by the wet beyond recognition. Zimmerman. He didn't know a Zimmerman. But here it was. Somebody's war medals, and a pouch of money, more than he'd ever seen. Chappie didn't count it. It wasn't his. The old teachings stayed with him, just below the surface of his skin. He stuffed everything back into the pouch, found a paper bag in the kitchen drawer and put the pouch in it. He went to the bedroom closet and stuffed it behind some boxes that hadn't been moved in years. He didn't know what he'd do with it, but he'd put it out of harm's way, before Annie came back and he had to show it to her, answer questions.

Chappie thought about the pouch for several days. He didn't take it out. He didn't want to know how much money was in it. He didn't want to be tempted by it. He wondered about Zimmerman. He asked Annie if she knew a Zimmerman. She didn't. When he stopped at Keenan's he asked about Zimmerman.

Jewish, probably, Keenan told him. Not around here. Ask at the bakery. They might know.

The following night Chappie stuffed the pouch in the pocket of the trousers he wore under his work overalls. He would go to the bakery and see if he could track down this Zimmerman. The pouch teased him with thoughts of the money inside: it wasn't his. He had to get rid of it before Annie stumbled on its hiding place in the closet. Then it might not be so easy to search for Zimmerman and get it back to its rightful owner. Throughout the night as he worked he'd touch the padded place under his overalls to assure himself it was still there. After work, despite being tired, he struck out to find Zimmerman. He wasn't sure why, just that he had to do it.

The bakery on Willard Avenue was a favorite stop when the family first moved to Friendship Street. It was a long walk, but Annie and the kids and Chappie went there with glee. He loved the yeasty smells and spices of wonderful bakery delights. They hadn't been there in a long time. He wondered briefly why they stopped coming.

He looked through the wide window filled with temptation. The store was painted blue and white, in need of a little touch up here and there, but just as inviting as when he first visited it. He opened the door; the bell attached to the door jingled a friendly welcome. He went inside breathing deep, inhaling the good sweet fragrance. He walked over to the row of display cases looking over the raisin squares, thick frosting coated cinnamon buns, rows and rows of bread, challah, raisin, rye, pumpernickel, and the simple thick sliced white bread Annie loved. She spread it with butter and jam with her tea. He pointed to a loaf, bought six raisin squares and four sugar cookies for the kids.

He was greeted and helped by a small thin man with gray hair and beard wearing an apron that touched the top of his shoes, his shirt a bright white with a starched collar. When he smiled his gold capped teeth gleamed and his blue eyes seemed to sparkle.

"You haven't been in for a while" the man said, "you and your wife and kinder."

Chappie smiled. "You have a good memory."

"You have a nice family, easy to remember."

"I'll have to bring them round soon," Chappie answered, flushing a bit at the remembrance.

"Zimmerman?" the old man looked across the counter at Chappie as he counted out the Chappie's change onto the dark table beside the display cases. The man's face was wrinkled and in the creases there were traces of white flour, like Chappie's own, lined with the coal dust from the trains, only black not white. "Why are you looking for Zimmerman? Is he Jewish?"

Chappie shrugged. "I have something of his to return to him. I don't know where he lives."

"Only Zimmerman I know runs the scrap yard on Point Street. Try there." The man folded Chappie's parcels almost lovingly, protecting the special goodness within. "It's cold outside," he said. "Package is warm. Say hello to the Missus for me."

Chappie nodded in response and took the two packages from the man and hugged them to his chest.

"Umm, warm," he said putting his nose against the bags and breathing deep. He smiled at the old man. "I'll be back. I'll bring the kids; it's been too long."

The scrap yard was two streets away and down about three blocks. It was cold, but Chappie had a mission. He didn't know why he was driven, but he was. The medals. He'd never had medals himself. He was no hero. Heroes got medals. It was nearly 10 o'clock. Annie would wonder where he was, not coming home from work right away. He wished they had a phone. He'd call her. Someday they'd get a phone. That would please Annie. It was always someday for Annie. He'd say someday, and she'd smile and nod her head, like she believed him. He thought she tried to believe him. It was so hard. So many times things went wrong, so many promises he didn't keep. He wiped his hand across his nose, and then held the packages closely. She'd like the bread and the raisin squares and cookies for the kids. It was a long time since he brought them anything.

The scrap yard was dingy; it was an old horse barn not needed for horses, reordered for a newer time. There were three stalls inside. The front door and plate glass window were stuck in where the barn door had been. The new door scraped the warped floor boards a little. Inside stalls were filled with old newspapers, pieces of metal and wood, and one was nearly up to the ceiling with broken parts of machines or house wares nobody needed. They'd be sold for the few pennies a pound to metal foundries, to be melted down, not for guns or tanks, but for refrigerators and new stoves and modern cars for a changing society.

The man looked up from the chair where he was sitting, an old leather book on his lap, a small lamp beside him casting a slight glow on the pages. He gestured with his head, asking without words, what do you want?

"Are you Zimmerman?" Chappie asked. The man stared at him, not sure, not ready to answer.

"I'm looking for Zimmerman," Chappie said. "That's all I know, just Zimmerman."

"There's lots of Zimmerman's" the man answered, his voice thick with an uncertain accent.

Chappie set his packages on the counter that separated the front of the small store from the stalls.

"Can I put these down?"The man gestured again with a nod of his head. "You've been to the bakery," he said, "my cousin's."

Chappie smiled and nodded his head. "I won't take much time. I'm tired, haven't been home from work yet," he said

"Trains? You work the trains? You got the cap and the pin." The man pointed to the blue cap and union pin Chappie wore everywhere. He almost wore it to church one Sunday when Annie asked him to go with him. They nearly had a big fight about the hat. He got out his soft hat, the brimmed gray fedora he bought years before when they were first married. The hat didn't suit him anymore. He did it for her. He wanted her to be happy. He just wasn't good at making it happen.

"Yeah," he said, "I work the night shift down at the yard."

"You're tired," he said, "so what do you want with Zimmerman?"

They both knew now this was Zimmerman. He was older than Chappie, maybe mid forties or more. Chappie wasn't good at age. "I found some things," Chappie said, hesitant for a bit. Suppose this was the wrong Zimmerman. He took the precious leather bag out of the paper sack. It was dry now, but stiff from being wet. He laid it on the counter and watched Zimmerman.

Zimmerman got up and went closer and as the satchel appeared from the bag he gave a small cry, like an animal might give if frightened suddenly, or like a child might.

"Where did you get that?" he asked pushing across the counter, his hand reaching as if to grab it away.

"You know what it is?" Chappie asked, covering it with his own large hand. That was how he'd know if this was the right Zimmerman. He'd know what was inside. He'd be able to describe it. He turned to look into Zimmerman's face. He was startled to see tears streaming down his face.

"Where did you find it?"

"Tell me what it is," Chappie answered.

The man sniffed and wiped the sleeve of his dirty gray and black plaid wool jacket across his mouth and nose. Chappie cringed seeing the whitish mucus clinging there.

"A minute," the man said, coughing, "a minute." His small but strong square shoulders convulsed. He took deep breaths gaining his composure after a few minutes and pulled a dark blue handkerchief from his pants pocket and wiped his nose and sleeve.

Chappie held his hand firmly on the leather pouch, keeping it safe a while longer. Things happen strangely in life. Zimmerman wrapped his arms around himself as if trying to hold himself together, ward off trembling. Chappie kept his eyes on the man. He wasn't that old: he looked old; his jacket was old, worn; his hands were stained with dirt and calloused, but not old, strong, not old. The smell of the metal and rust and remnants of the old barn, rotting wood assaulted Chappie's lungs in the air he breathed. This place would make anyone old. He felt a sudden closeness to this man, wanted to reach out, embrace him like he might cuddle his little son. Of course, he could not.

Zimmerman straightened up, lifted his head higher projecting dignity. "Where did you get this?" he repeated his earlier question but more firmly now. "Why did you bring it to me?"

"The baker said you are the only Zimmerman he knows; you go to his temple. He didn't say you were his cousin. The paper inside is some kind of document, not English. I thought I'd check here first."

"It's German," he said, "the language on the card, German." His eyes riveted on Chappie to see what his next move would be.

"German," Chappie repeated. "Is it yours?"

"It belonged to my father, his card, his medals, from the war, the other one…

Chappie nodded his head. "What else is in the pouch?"

The man stared at him. "Some money, my father's medals, his old army card, a letter and a jewel from my mother. That's all. Nothing is left of his life, of her life. All gone." Tear began to glisten in his eyes again.

Chappie took his hand away from the pouch. German medals from the other war, World War I, money, a lot of money, American money. Chappie thought he could have thrown the pouch away, medals and all, and kept the money. What did this man need of that, German things, Germans here in the neighborhood? He looked at the pouch for a minute then pushed it away, like it was hot, contaminated; it stopped against Zimmerman's hand resting on the counter. Slowly Zimmerman let his fingers of his right hand reach for the pouch, touch it, move on top of it, close over it.

"I thought it was gone forever. Maybe it doesn't matter anymore; everything else is gone."

He looked at Chappie as if he recognized a stranger in his shop, a man who should be greeted, invited to sit. He'd forgotten his manners. He gestured, "Come in, come sit."

Chappie looked up at the clock; it was getting on toward eleven. Annie would wonder where he was.

"I only wanted to get it to the rightful owner. I found it in the gutter, under some leaves that dammed the rain water. I'm sorry it got wet. I was going home, feeling blue and kicked the leaves to let the water flow. There it was."

"Come and sit. I want to tell you about my father, my family, maybe for the last time. They are all gone now."

"I should go home," Chappie said. "You just take the pouch. Maybe I'll come again. My wife is waiting." Chappie gestured to the bags he'd set on the table.

"You are a lucky man, a wife, a family maybe?"

Chappie nodded assent. "I guess I am," Chappie said. There was something more here. He wanted to stay and hear more, but he knew he had to go home; he had to leave Zimmerman with the fragments of a life gone. He didn't know the details. He didn't want to, not then. Annie was expecting him home.

"It's a lot of money, almost $1200. You could have kept it, not come looking." Zimmerman seemed to see Chappie for the first time, a working man like himself, younger, harsher maybe, troubled from the expression on his face, a drinker, Zimmerman thought.

"I don't keep what isn't mine," Chappie answered.

As if to hold on to the moment longer Zimmerman continued talking. "It was passage money for my father. I tried to bring him here. It was too late. They are all gone, mother, sisters, brothers, all killed in the war, Jewish, you know. My father was the only one left, but I couldn't get him out of Germany. He survived the camps. He died before he could come here, red tape, too long a wait, too sick to travel. His heart was broken. He sent me these things. This is all I have, all he had to send me. Not the money; that was his too. I saved it to bring him here. Once he died it was dirty to me, my failure."

Zimmerman had strung all the words together rapidly, as if he needed to have Chappie hear the story quickly, as if it was the only time he would be able to tell him, and Chappie was trying to leave, go home. He continued on, "My father's son failed him. I was in England before the war studying. My friends and my father made me stay, afraid I'd be killed. They were killing Jews in Germany you know."

Chappie knew. Everyone knew. Chappie stopped him, put up his hand as if holding off a line of traffic in the street. Stop.

"I have to go home," he said.

"Take the money," Zimmerman said.

Chappie shook his head. No. He could not take this man's money. He wished he had never found the pouch. He wished it had washed down the sewer with the rainwater. It brought pain. He saw pain in Zimmerman's face. His own stomach was knotted with sadness.

"I'm sorry. I shouldn't have come here."

"Yes, you were right to come" Zimmerman said. "You've given me something of my life back. Someday I'll tell you the story."

Chappie gathered the bags from the bakery. Zimmerman followed him to the door.

"Thank you…" he paused. "I don't know your name."

"Chappie," he answered. "I come from Friendship Street."

"A good name for a street," Zimmerman said. He looked around turning his head this way and that as if he were trying to find something in the cluttered shop. "I want to give you something for your wife."

"No," Chappie said. He held the bags close to him as he walked out the door, Zimmerman holding it open with one hand, his pouch in the other.

When he returned home Annie was angry and the bread crushed. The cookies and fig bars survived. He didn't tell her about Zimmerman, or the money he found and returned. He wanted to think she'd be proud of him, but she might think he failed her once again. Maybe she'd think the money was a gift from heaven, a sign that things could be different. He just didn't trust her, didn't trust she believed in the good man he used to be, and didn't want to give her one more disappointment.

About two weeks after Chappie returned the pouch Zimmerman turned up on his front porch. Annie answered the bell. Zimmerman was dressed in a worn navy blue top coat, his beard trimmed, face shaved and washed, what was left of his graying brown hair was combed back and slicked down, his soft dress hat in his hand.

She looked at him a little fearfully, "Yes?" It was her way of addressing someone she didn't know, with trepidation.

"Is Chappie home?" he asked. He extended his hand. "I'm Zimmerman, his friend."

Annie hesitated a little then smiled. A friend calling for Chappie. Annie never knew any of Chappie's friends; none had ever called at the house.

"He's sleeping," she answered.

"Oh, yes, I forgot," Zimmerman said hesitating. "I forgot he works at night.""He'll be up soon," she said. "He gets up at seven to have time with the children. I can tell him you are here."Zimmerman shook his head. No. He lifted the white bakery bag in his left hand and pushed it toward her. "For the children," he said, "sugar cookies from my cousin's bakery. And white bread to go with your jam. Please tell Chappie I called."

"Do you want to come in?" she asked almost as an afterthought as she took the bags from him."Just tell him Zimmerman stopped by to say hello," he said and turned and quickly ran down the porch stairs putting his hat on. Annie didn't know it, but those few moments were life changing for her. This small Jewish man held her future in his hands and in his heart.

Chappie was surprised when Annie told him about Zimmerman's visit and the sugar cookies and the thick white bakery bread. "I wonder how he found us," he said. "I didn't tell him where we lived."

"I asked around," Zimmerman told him when Chappie visited him at his shop the next morning on the way home from work. He told Annie he was going to stop by and see Zimmerman.

"He's a nice man," Chappie said. He avoided any more questions about Zimmerman.

"He said he was your friend," she said. "Yes," Chappie said surprised at the comment.

"He isn't a drinker is he?"

"No," Chappie answered, surprised yet not really surprised at her question, maybe just a little hurt. "Just a friend."

Stopping by Zimmerman's place became a once in a while thing. Chappie liked Zimmerman. Zimmerman wanted to talk to him about his family, about living in Germany as a boy, and England where he went to school as a young man. His father knew what was ahead and wanted his son to be safe. He sent him away. It was one of Zimmerman's heartbreaks that he wasn't with his family when they were taken away to the camps.

"Maybe I could have helped them, saved them even," he told Chappie.

"No," Chappie answered, seeing the pain in his friend's face, "nobody could save anyone then; you would have been killed."

The anguish kept Zimmerman from a normal life. His cousin brought him to America from England so he could be close to the only family he had left. He never married though his cousin often tried to find a suitable bride for him. Zimmerman bought the scrap business and it became his whole life. Sometimes he visited his cousin's family, mostly at holiday time.

"It's no good, though," he told Chappie, "too many memories."

Zimmerman taught Chappie how to play chess. After a while Annie asked Chappie to bring Zimmerman for supper; it became a regular thing. Often he brought his violin to play for the family. He talked about his young years when his family all played music together. He bought violins for Chappie's girls and older boy and began to teach them how to play; the baby was too young, but he loved the sounds of music and danced in circles when anyone played.

Zimmerman gave Chappie money to buy Annie a piano. She played as a young girl, but hadn't in years. One day a truck came to the house. The driver said he was to deliver a small spinet to their address. Annie at first turned it away, but when she realized Chappie's name was on the delivery slip she knew Zimmerman must have sent it to the family. She let the men to put it in the parlor. She began to play old songs she'd remembered from her girlhood when the Sisters at the Catholic School taught the girls music in the basement of the church.

Zimmerman brought his old pictures to show the family, snapshots and a few tintypes of his grandparents, his parents and brothers and sisters and himself as a young man. Annie gave him an album and they sat around the round dinner table pasting pictures into the book for him. He left it on the piano for a while.

Zimmerman was better for Chappie than the priest. He worked every day growing his scrap business, adding new items for the increasing market of new home owners who were learning the art of do it yourself. He and Chappie talked when they played chess; he told Chappie about the old country, his family and his losses. He told Chappie he was destroying himself and his family with drink. He taught Chappie that what mattered in all the world was family, not by lecturing him, but by sharing his personal grief. Also, he encouraged Chappie to help out at the scrap shop on Saturdays.

Zimmerman became like an older brother to him, closer, more helpful than his own brothers were.

Annie tried to find some of Zimmerman's relatives. She talked with his cousin at the bakery when she went there on her own to buy bread and cinnamon rolls. She got in touch with the refugee help organizations, but they had no luck. Zimmerman was right. When they realized there was no family besides his cousin, who was, in fact a very distant cousin, they adopted Zimmerman as their own. They invited his cousin and wife to supper now and again where the conversation, out of earshot of Zimmerman, often wandered to finding him a wife. Annie and Chappie and the cousin entered into a conspiracy of sorts to find Zimmerman a bride. There was a woman working at the bakery who was perfect, a nice Jewish girl, Miriam, the cousin said. Though Zimmerman went to his cousin's bakery from time to time it was generally early in the morning and if he saw the woman they never spoke. With Annie, Chappie and the cousin and his wife helping, they introduced the two. She was thirty two, younger than Zimmerman, but old enough. Annie had a dinner where the two met, with Zimmerman's cousin and his wife joining in to give approval. It wasn't long before a wedding took place.

Zimmerman moved out of the rooms behind the scrap shop. He bought a large tenement house in the Jewish neighborhood not too far away from Friendship Street, close enough to her family and friends; close enough to the bakery so she could continue to work.

"A tenement house always pays," he told Chappie. "If something happens to me, God forbid, Miriam will have the rents to help her through."

Chappie changed through his experiences with Zimmerman. He began to rebuild himself. He saw the joy Zimmerman found in Miriam and, in a short while, his new son. He told Chappie he now had a reason to be prosperous. He was working for his family and for their future.

"It's what you have, what you've had for a long time," Zimmerman told Chappie. "You just didn't appreciate it, dumb ox you are!"

Once married the visits between Chappie and Zimmerman were less frequent. Chappie missed him. Miriam began to work with Zimmerman at the scrap shop on Saturday, so Chappie stopped. When the families came together it was different. They didn't play music as much, or play chess as much. Sometimes Chappie stopped by the scrap shop to play chess. It was on one of these days that Zimmerman introduced Chappie to his new plan, to help Chappie buy a house.

It was a bittersweet subject for Chappie. He told Zimmerman of his failure during the war, not being able to serve in the military, not earning the right to have a GI Bill house. Unknown to Chappie, when the opportunity came up, Zimmerman purchased the tenement Chappie lived in with his family. Chappie knew there was a new owner, a real estate company. Annie was annoyed they had to buy a money order and mail the rent to a business office instead of paying cash to the old man who owned the house previously. It was more than a year before Zimmerman told Chappie he bought the tenement.

"I used the $1200," he said, "and the money you wouldn't take for working at the shop on Saturdays. I invested it and it earned well. It is really your money, so I decided the house is really yours."

Chappie refused. "That was your father's money, your money."

"You can't refuse," Zimmerman said. "It is in Annie's name. It's for her and your family."

Chappie's face flushed red. "You cannot give a house to my wife," he said angrily.

"You wouldn't take the money you found when you needed it and I didn't. Now you won't take the value the money has earned." Zimmerman got up from his chair where he and Chappie were playing chess.

"You are my brother. You are my only relative besides my wife and son and my cousin. You gave me back my life."

Chappie stared at Zimmerman. "You gave me back my life," Chappie countered. "You saved me from the drink; you gave me my family back. We're even."

"Your brother Zimmerman is giving you the house purchased with the money you found and wouldn't keep. Do you understand goodness? Do you understand you must let me give you something for all you and Annie have done for me?"

So it was that the apartment house on Friendship Street was given to Chappie and Annie, though Annie knew nothing of the gift. It was a secret between the "brothers." Chappie and Zimmerman continued to invest together. The money Chappie used to spend on drink was set aside, his allowance, and he gave it to Zimmerman for their building fund. The rents from the house tenants were used to pay the mortgage, including Chappie's rent which Annie continued to mail to a rental agent every month. Things were better for Chappie's family now that he wasn't drinking. Day by day things went on as usual.

"You have to tell Annie," Zimmerman told Chappie. "You have to tell her you bought her a house, an investment."

At first Chappie declined. Somewhere in his soul was the sense that the house wasn't really his, that sooner or later he'd give it back to Zimmerman.

"I have no need of it; I have three tenements now, and we own another together through our investments," Zimmerman told him. "You may not need this house, but Annie does. You have to do this for her."

It was near Christmas in 1952 when Chappie came home from work with shopping bags full of Christmas lights and decorations. Annie was surprised. It was not like him to make merry the holidays. It was more like him to sit back, drink a coffee and watch her and the kids put the Christmas together.

"I want it to different this year," he told her. The kids dug into the bags and spread the packages out on the long dining room table, excited about their finds.

"Why different?" Annie asked. What was up? She was suspicious.

"Wait and see," he answered. "And let's have the family for

Christmas Eve. I know they won't want to come on Christmas Day since Benny and Marilyn always do Christmas Day at their place. The Zimmerman's will come for Christmas. "

"This year is different." Chappie still had his coat on and went out onto the circular porch that dressed the front of the tall house. There were two doors, one into the main floor, where they lived, and the second off to the side to the second and third floor tenements. All the apartments were rented. Chappie helped the owner, who he only recently learned was Zimmerman, find the tenants, making sure they were what he called good people. Four tenant families lived upstairs, two middle aged couples on the second floor, and two young couples with two babies each on the third, and four renters in single rooms. Zimmerman had Chappie collect their rent and made sure it was paid on time, except for Chappie's rent which Annie mailed. Zimmerman paid Chappie a little, putting it into their investment fund, for watching the place, making sure the garbage was put out on time, and doing some of the odd jobs around to keep the place in good order. He didn't tell Annie about that. Chappie did such a good job of upkeep on the place that it was one of the best looking houses on Friendship Street, except for maybe the Greek's place up the street that was newer and had only one large extended family living in it. The tenement house was a good and profitable little business.

"Someday maybe I can buy this place from you," Chappie told Zimmerman when he first learned Zimmerman owned the house. "When you get ready to sell let me the place let me know he told Zimmerman once, "and maybe I'll be in a place to talk about buying."

That was four years back just after Zimmerman married; he offered Chappie the chance to take care of the house. Chappie got through his anger about not being able to have the GI Bill. Some of the trainmen and a few other guys, a couple of merchant marines who were in the same boat, talked about forcing the government to give the GI Bill to men who weren't allowed to serve, but who had to stay on essential and sometimes dangerous jobs throughout the war, not allowed to quit even to enlist.

"Naw," he said as the talk went on, "I'll make my own," And that's what he tried to do, investing some of his earnings with Zimmerman when there was an old tenement needing repair on the market. Chappie, with Zimmerman's instruction, learned to paint and repair and used some of his work effort as part of his share of buying the place. Someday he would buy Annie a home.

Christmas was beautiful that year. The city was blanketed with snow. Marilyn called to say she wasn't sure they'd make it Christmas Eve if the snow didn't let up. It did though. And they did arrive with their kids. Chappie had a new car, a used Chrysler sedan; he drove over to the old neighborhood with Annie to pick up her mother. When Nana got to the side of the car, just before Chappie opened the door for her, she ran her gloved hand across the navy blue door. "Pretty car," she said.

When they approached the house on Friendship Street the red and green and yellow lights were gleaming and patterned on the narrow strip of snow covered grass in front of the house. Single electric candles shone in all the downstairs windows. Lights were strung across the front porch on the railings and just below the second floor ledge. It was a lovely sight. Chappie had hung a Christmas wreath on each of the doors. It made Annie proud that they had all worked hard to have a lovely Christmas.

They planned to go to Midnight Mass at the Cathedral all together. It had been years since they'd done that. Marilyn and Benny begged off Midnight Mass; their children needed to be home in their beds for Santa Claus' visit. Good. That was good, Chappie thought.

For Christmas Eve dinner there was wonderful roast beef. Turkey was for Thanksgiving. Annie had slaved over her cooking. It had been a few years since the whole family sat around their table to celebrate. The table gleamed with new China dishes Chappie and Annie picked out . They were white with deep maroon bands and flowers in the center. There were side plates and bowls and serving bowls, all of which Annie set out with her two daughters helping. The large serving bowls were filled with mashed potatoes and carrots and sweet peas and home baked rolls. There was more food than needed. The buffet, a hand me down from Chappie's mother years ago before she died, was filled with pies and cakes. They were from Zimmerman's cousin's Jewish bakery on Willard Avenue, always delicious.

For the food was eaten with must gusto, then dessert and coffee. Chappie didn't offer any drinks. He toasted the family with apple cider.

"My gift to you all, I've given up the drink," he said, holding his glass high. There was laughing, like maybe he was joking. Surely, he was joking. But Annie knew, and for Chappie that was what mattered.

Annie invited everyone to the living room around the tree. Gifts were assembled there for all the guests. Kids would get their gifts in the morning, like all the kids did. Each adult received a beautifully wrapped gift.

"The department store did it," Annie said, as she passed them out, a little embarrassed by the fancy ribbons and paper.

"You must have won big on the horses," Benny said. "The railroad doesn't pay this good."

"The railroad pays pretty good," he said to Benny, "enough to save a little to treat the family."

The gifts were well suited to everyone, shirts, sweaters, gloves, blouses. All were appreciated. There were two boxes remaining.

"One for you, Nana," Chappie said. He handed a small box to Annie's mother. He gave another to Annie. "Annie, open your gift first."

Annie fumbled with the small box Jewelry? No. He never bought her jewelry, not even an engagement ring. There was no money for that then. Maybe now. She tore the package away and took out a small Christmas card.

"To Annie," the front of the card read. She opened it. There was a small picture of the house, their tenement house. She looked puzzled.

"Look on the back," he said.

She turned it over. It read: To Annie, her own house from my own GI Bill. Love, Chappie.

"Now, Mama," he said to Annie's mother, "open yours."

It was a key. The card read: "Your own house key to our home, and a welcome forever. Thank you for all you've done for your family, Love, Chappie.

There was silence. Annie stared at the photo. Her mother stared at the key. Nobody oohed or ahhed the way they had when they'd all gone to Marilyn's and Benny's open house. Nobody said congratulations. Annie let tears stream down her face. Annie's mother tucked her own personal key in her pocket, telling them all that it was nice that she had invitations to stay at both of her daughter's homes if she ever needed to. Chappie allowed himself a brief image of his mother-in-law sharing a room with one of the kids in the tiny bedrooms at Marilyn's and Benny's. Or maybe they'd let her sleep on the pullout couch in the lately finished basement playroom. He smiled inwardly. He had an extra bedroom for Ma if she ever needed it, and a better car than Benny, and the respect of the whole neighborhood. He felt an inward pleasure.

It was nearly time for Mass. Everyone chattered and admired their gifts. They said goodbyes to Benny and Marilyn and the kids, bundling the nieces and nephews warmly, and putting their still wrapped gifts into sacks for their journey home. Then everyone put on coats and hats and gloves to prepare for Mass. Annie still held her picture. Tears were glistening in her eyes.

"How did you do this?" she asked him.

"Very quietly," he answered. "I knew we had both lost many things through the years, our pride, our caring for each other, and our vision of a future. I wanted it back, here, together. I had a choice and I chose you."

He told her how Zimmerman helped, how they were real estate partners, that there would be money for the kids for school and someday if she wanted to move out of the neighborhood they could leave Friendship Street.

"Never," she answered smiling, tears pouring down her face.

The Zimmerman's came to celebrate Christmas. Early in December Annie and Chappie and the kids had gone to Zimmerman's for the festival of the lights, Hanukah. It was a joyful family tradition now, happiness Zimmerman never expected, and he shared it with his new brother and his family.

Very few people knew the story of Chappie's own GI Bill. What they knew was the family living in the big Victorian was a good family. They were helping people. Annie worked hard to bring good things to the community at the center. Chappie helped organize fireworks on the 4th of July and in his own way helped families in trouble, a little money, maybe food, or help finding a job. There was a lot of trouble on Friendship Street. He knew that. He'd known his own kind of trouble and found his way through. He knew and Annie knew they were lucky. They used their luck to make Friendship Street a better place, and their home a light in the neighborhood.

Survival and Saying Goodbye

It was Jenny's first day working in the jewelry factory. High school graduation two weeks earlier was just a memory. Jenny's mother and her Nana sat on the folding chairs set up in the auditorium and watched Jenny accept her graduation certificate from the principal. After there was a small celebration with punch and cookies in the gymnasium and chats with students' families or faculty and their spouses, most of whom were strangers to Jenny. She didn't get honors, but she did pass all her classes with A grades except penmanship and typing, which she was required to take because her counselor was convinced she would have to take a job and without typing and writing skills what could she do? Jenny and her mother and Nana walked to the bus stop. Nana was going home and Jenny with her; her mother was going to work. Is that all there is? Jenny thought, a sense of nothingness followed the ceremony, a sense that all the work she'd done, the grades she'd earned were for naught.

She was accepted at the college of education, where she could live at home and walk downtown and under the wide railroad bridge to classes every day. It was the only college she applied to for admittance. Nobody told Jenny until later, after she attended for a year and knew she had to leave, that she had scored highest on entrance examinations than all other students except for one, and he decided not to attend the college. He got a scholarship to an Ivy League college. Jenny didn't have any scholarships, and didn't know anything about how one got money for college. Jenny's mother was surprised they let her in to the college at all, since they lived on Friendship Street, and people from poor places didn't get to go to college.

"Don't be disappointed if they send you a letter that you can't go there," her mother told her.

But the letter didn't say that. It said congratulations and come to class orientation in mid September. She needed money for college; about two hundred dollars for student fees and the same amount for books. It wasn't a lot, but she needed to earn money that summer to be able to pay the fees. There was no family money, no rich uncle, or anyone who cared enough that she'd earned the honor of going to college. So, when her Aunt Irene told her mother one of the factories was looking for girls, Jenny's mother was excited. Irene was Uncle Edmund's wife, an unpleasant enough woman, who was always looking for gossip to spread and never had a good word for anyone.

"You can start here. Who knows, you might like it and earn enough so you won't want to go to college after all," her mother said. Her dream for Jenny was she'd get a job and meet somebody with a good job and get married and live happily ever after. It was the theme of the movies her mother and sometimes her dad and kids went to on Wednesday nights and Sunday matinees. There were musicals and drama. Nobody liked the dark side of films, mysteries or some of the B-movies used to fill out the schedules. There were always two movies, mostly paired so the venue was positive and wholesome and alright for the kids to see. There were lessons in those movies: life could be good and happy and you could sing and dance through it and forget the bad stuff.

For Jenny factory jobs meant Friendship Street. It meant staying on a trodden path she'd seen too much of; it fed her fear of never being able to get away from the pattern of life of poor people, forgotten people, desperate people whose lives churned on and on with the same cadence. It frightened her, staying forever on Friendship Street. She wanted more. She expected more of herself.

Despite her misgivings Jenny agreed to apply for the job at the jewelry factory. She could have applied for an office slot the hiring boss told her because she had a high school diploma. But Jenny said no, she didn't want to work where she had to dress up each day in a skirt and blouse and hose. She only had one set of dress clothes that would suit for the job. She wanted to be more casual and not use money earned to buy outfits for the office. She was assigned a job as an order picker. She'd have a list to follow and was shown around the factory floor to learn the number layouts and how to most efficiently follow the list. It seemed dumb work to Jenny, boring, but at least she wasn't sitting at a punch press where you could only get up two times in the morning and two times in the afternoon for breaks, and the women doing the job complained of back aches and took aspirin washed down with Cokes to get through the day..

It wasn't a bad place to work. Aunt Irene told her it was one of the better factories where the company had a coffee and muffin layout in the morning and Cokes and pretzels in the afternoon. There was half an hour for lunch, and if you didn't mind be frisked coming and going you could carry your lunch out to the park across the street and eat on the benches there. The friskings were at the end of the shift or any time you left the plant. They were humiliating, Jenny thought. They were done so the girls didn't steal the jewelry. They were all called girls, even the white haired old ladies who had worked their whole lives in factories. They laughed and made bawdy remarks when the men at the gates ran their hands ups and down their slacks and blouses to check for contraband. Who would steal the awful stuff they made? Glossy glass beads or broaches with fake glass jewels dipped in fake gold or silver.

One of the rights of passage was stealing a piece of jewelry. The crabby voiced woman, her name badge read Babs, with salt and pepper hair told Jenny that. Everyone who wanted to work in the shop had to do that. If you didn't it would be reported to the bosses that you did steal and then you'd be in for it.

"Don't mess with me," the woman told Jenny. "If we report you stealing you'll go to jail."

"I'm Catholic," Jenny responded, "and I can't steal; it's a sin."

The woman harrumphed. "You better not come back to work in the morning. All the girls who work here take a few pieces. You get to keep one or two, but you bring me three or more. The more, the better you'll get along. We're counting on you." She looked Jenny up and down.

"I can't do that..." Jenny began.

"Yeah, you can. You got those nice big boobies. You just whisk some pieces down there, and there you have it. You can do it." The woman waved her arm over her head like a farewell to Jenny and walked down the aisle and disappeared around the corner. Jenny didn't see her again that day.

Jenny finished her day and then, passing through the frisking she walked through the clutch of people on the sidewalk outside the factory and headed home. A few people smiled at her but mostly she was ignored as she headed up the hill to go home. Her head was abuzz. What could she do? If she didn't go to work she wouldn't have money to go to college. If she didn't work her mother couldn't give her money to pay her fees. She was on her own. Her mom and dad said they would help her by providing food and a place to live, but even that was stretching it for them. Her father hoped she'd get a job and pay board like he remembered doing when he was young, and the way her sister was paying board. Her sister didn't have any high brow ideas about going to college.

"Don't think you're too high and mighty to work in a shop," her Aunt Irene told her. Irene had spent more than twenty years in different factories, on piece work, she'd tell anyone who'd listen. She claimed she earned more than a secretary or school teacher doing piece work: working with her head down over her stamping machine as the pieces were rushed through faster than fast. No time for a break, no time to chat with the workers down the line. Every minute was money made. To Jenny it sounded bleak.

"It's back breaking," her mother told her, "working like that. The money's not worth it to me."

Jenny debated whether she'd tell her mother about the stealing going on. She wasn't sure what her response would be. She wanted to think her mother would commend her for not stealing. She thought she would. But she just didn't trust the outcomes. She felt her mother was already disappointed she wanted to go to college. To let her think she couldn't fit in with a simple summer job would undermine her faith in Jenny.

She fretted on it late into the night, and the next morning when the alarm rang and Jenny got up, ate toast and tea, and dressed for work she didn't have a chance to talk to her mother. Her mother worked a 3 to 11 shift at the rubber plant. She wasn't home before Jenny went to bed, and she was still sleeping when Jenny left for work. She had to go to work. It was expected. Slowly Jenny headed down Pine Street and down the side streets to the factory. She stood outside for a few minutes, hearing the morning bell that told her she was late. She went inside, clocked in, put her lunch and purse in the small locker assigned to her, and went to her cubby where the packing lists for the day waited on her table.

The foreman came by checking on her. "You're late," he said. "Don't make a habit of it or you'll be docked an hour's pay." Seeing she was settled in the foreman continued on his rounds.

The stack of orders she was expected to complete that morning was tall. She worked fast, and instead of getting praise for that she just got more lists. Each list was an order for an assortment of jewelry pieces to be packed into a shipping box, the box sealed with brown tape, the label affixed and it set on the long table at the end of the row for the shipping boy to pick it up. The only talk that went on was in the girls bathroom, where people took breaks on three plastic sofas and a couple of tables. The talk there was who was married, who was newly engaged, and who was having the next wedding or baby shower. The conversations were not pleasant, and except for one other quiet woman, Ernestine, probably close to forty years old, Jenny didn't have much interest in talking. During the fifteen minute break time she ate her bun and drank tea and listened while Ernestine talked about her three kids in Catholic school. Jenny puzzled, watching the different women, wondering if they stole like she was told to do. She couldn't imagine Ernestine stealing.

Jenny didn't see the woman Babs who wanted her to steal that day or for two of the following days. Once when she saw her headed into the girls room Jenny turned and went back to her station. She thought about how she might get around stealing. She wondered if everyone did it, and almost talked with Ernestine about it, but was afraid to mention it. Ernestine was a good catholic woman. Did she steal? Maybe she did then went to Confession and was absolved of the sin.

Jenny was in her fourth day at the factory when Babs came up behind her as she was filling one of the order boxes.

"How's things?" Babs asked.

Jenny shrugged, "Going okay."

"I didn't see you looking me up with your offering," Babs said.

Jenny stared at her. Babs was running her hands through a shelf of green glass turtle broaches. She picked one up and handed it to Jenny.

"Now this is just what I have in mind," she said. "Ain't it pretty? Maybe two of these could be passed to me at afternoon break." She smiled a phony smile. "You can do this."

Jenny stood in front of the shelf, still holding the green turtle in her hand. She saw the foreman at the end of the line and put the turtle in the order box as she watched him come toward her.

"How's things girlie?" he asked. He called everyone girlie or babe. There were too many girls to remember them all.

Jenny closed the lid on the box, as if it was just finished.

"Good," she answered, "going good."

He smiled and walked on. "You'll get used to things round here," he answered.

Jenny felt sweat on her brow. She wondered if he was in on the stealing, if he claimed some of the pieces the girls stole. She passed her hand across her forehead and wiped it on her slack. She felt sick to her stomach. She just wanted to leave, go home. At the end of the row she took the turtle out of the box and slid it into her slacks pocket. She couldn't go back down the row and put it on the shelf. No turning back. The lists were in order. You could only go one way down the row. If she turned and went back it would be noticed. She sealed the order box, attached the label and went on to the next row, the next order. She did it over and over until all her lists were filled. She counted the stack of completed orders boxed, wrote the number on top of the stack and went to the break room for her fifteen minute time out. She walked past the toilets and on to one of the corner tables where she sat down. She out her head down on her folded arms.

Ernestine came up beside her. "Are you okay, Jenny?" she asked her.

"I feel sick to my stomach," Jenny said lifting her head to meet her eyes.

"Go to the nurse," Ernestine told her. "They'll send you home early."

Jenny leapt at the opportunity to leave the break room, hearing Babs' voice in the background. Ernestine lead her down the corridor just before the office where the nurse's room was. She went inside with her until Jenny was checked in by the nurse and asked to sit down on the bench. She sat. As she did so she brushed her hand against the small lump in her pocket. The turtle. What would she do? When she went out she'd be frisked. She felt sheer terror overtake her and began to shake. Her stomach whirled and she thought she'd vomit. The nurse, realizing her distress headed her to the toilet. She didn't need the toilet but sat on the stool.

"Are you okay?" she called through the closed stall.

"Yeah," Jenny responded. "I'll be right out."

Jenny reached into her pocket and tucked the turtle in her bra, securing it with a wad of toilet paper. Then she went out

"I've written you an excuse so you can go home early," the nurse said. "Do you need a ride home?"

No. No ride home. Just let me out of here.

"I'll walk you out," the nurse said. "You don't need those doormen poking you about." Did she know? Had this happened to other young women? Jenny nodded in response, followed the nurse while she walked Jenny to get her purse and sweater from the check in locker, then, waving her paper excuse, walked Jenny to the front door. Front door, imagine that. She didn't have to go through the side door where the doormen were at end of the day.

"They aren't there except at closing and lunch," the nurse told her. She smiled as she saw Jenny out the door onto the front sidewalk.

Suddenly the air was clean and fresh. Jenny breathed in deeply and took a long look at the tall factory. She put her hand against her chest and felt the wad of paper concealing the turtle. Still there. She didn't know what to do with it. She thought of tossing it into the gutter or in a bush but she was convinced she might be seen and pounced on. She walked slowly up the hill to Friendship Street. Nothing seemed right to her. She'd stolen from her employer. What could she do now? If they knew she could be arrested. The thought overwhelmed her. She wouldn't be allowed to go to college. Maybe she'd go to jail. Her stomach was lurching again. She'd go see Nana.

Jenny walked to the Broad Street Trolley stop where she caught the trolley up to the stop at the top of Pavilion Avenue. She jumped off in her usual chipper way when she thought about seeing her Nana. She'd have an answer. She'd know what to do, always did.

Years later when Jenny thought of Nana she remembered this special day. She went down the hill from the trolley stop. She was eager to see Nana but she had a heavy heart. Her Nana's arms wrapped her around.

"Look who's here in the middle of the work day," she said. "Looks like you're running from the Banshee." Running from the mythical Irish creature that howled of death she meant. "But it can't be as bad as that."

Jenny sat at the table as Nana made the tea and added some crackers and jam to the feast.

"Now then," she said, sitting opposite Jenny.

And Jenny collapsed sobbing her tale of theft and fear and how she might be arrested and couldn't go back to the factory.

"You shouldn't have been there in the first place," Nana said, high school diploma and all. "And it isn't like you'd planned to steal the turtle. After all, what is it, a glass bob, a nothing to worry about."

Nana made it all easy. She put things into perspective.

Jenny felt her stomach ease, the warm milky sugary tea, and the jam and crackers comforted her. Jenny pulled the turtle from its place in her bra and put it on the table.

Nana covered the sparkly green turtle with tiny red glass eyes with her hand.

"A nice piece," she said, "but not worth all this turmoil. We'll just send it back."

Nana found a little cardboard box and with Jenny's help they tucked the turtle inside. Nana wrote a letter to the President of the factory and put it in the box.

"I'll mail it off for you," she said.

Nothing more was said of it. Jenny did not return to the factory. There was nothing to be gained by that. Jenny stayed overnight at Nana's, and in the morning the whole world was brighter.

"I have to earn money," Jenny said when she came down to her breakfast of tea and cinnamon toast.

"Well, I've thought about that," she said. "Mrs. Hadley up the street is in need of help with her kids this summer. And I told her you were available to do child care five hours a day for a reasonable rate. So we'll go up and have a cuppa with her and work it all out."

So they did. And about a week later Nana received a letter from the President of jewelry company expressing regrets about Jenny's experience at the factory. He asked Jenny and Nana to come by and visit him at his office so he could express his support for Jenny's unwillingness to participate in stealing at the company. The following week Nana and Jenny went to meet with him.

"You can come back to work and take the office job we originally offered," he said during their meeting.

Jenny declined.

"She's got a good summer job taking care of Mrs. Hadley's kids, and she's going to college in the fall," Nana told him.

The President thanked Jenny and also thanked her Nana. He told them Jenny's experiences and her refusing to steal and Nana's letter lead them to an investigation and disciplining people who caused the problem. He was sure Jenny helped the company save money, and made the work environment better for workers. Just before he left he presented Jenny with a check for $300 to help with her college fees.

Jenny learned many lessons from her short work experience that summer. She learned about the importance of values. She learned the strength of saying no to something that was wrong. And most of all she learned to trust her family, to bring troubles home where the power of the family could help solve big problems.

Jenny's mother was relieved when Jenny and Nana told her about the outcomes of the factory job. That summer Jenny stayed overnight at Nana's during the work week to make it easier to do her childcare job. Jenny gained new faith in her mother, and best of all, she had enough money to start college in the fall. It wasn't all sunlight and roses, but it was better. When

Jenny went off to her first day at college she had the sense that the women of her family, especially her Nana and her mom had her back.

For Jenny the factory experience was about survival. There was a big world beyond Friendship Street, and while she wasn't sure she was ready to take it on, she knew she could not stay still and immoveable. She had to go forward. The factory experience taught her that going forward meant relying upon the lessons she'd learned through the years on Friendship Street, and the teaching of her family. There was a steadiness in that.

Not long after the factory experiences Jenny's family moved from the basement apartment on Friendship Street to a large third floor flat on Point Street. It was down again, further south from Pavilion Avenue, but the neighborhood was better, more steady, larger flats, not apartments, and though they were renting, many families owned their own homes. Her mother said now there was a college girl in the family they needed to have a better place to live, for all of them. Jenny had her own room, a rarity throughout her life, but important since she was studying at home while going to college. The new flat was closer to the college and the walk was shorter.

The goodbye to Friendship Street was unnoticed. Nobody came out to say goodbye or offered any celebration. There was little regret at their leaving, and maybe just a bit of jealousy. The family had little to move, since the basement apartment was furnished. The few boxes of dishes and clothes and small items like lamps and pictures, a few books and pots and pans all went into small boxes and were moved in Uncle Franks' car. Jenny's dad had a dream of his own car, and that would come in a little while. The move away from Friendship Street was hopeful, like a new beginning. It was the right time to say goodbye, before the children grew and moved away. That would happen in the next few years. But for now they were together in a better place, going forward. It had taken longer than Jenny's mother hoped, but at last, Friendship Street with all its lessons and losses was behind them. Nana was happy for them and bought a housewarming gift for the new home, a new coffee percolator and a fruit patterned table cloth. It went along with the new furniture, well, mostly second hand new furniture, her mom and dad shopped for and had moved to the new flat. Among the purchases was a cherry wood bookcase with sliding glass doors, filled with the books from a lawyer who had died. The books thrilled Jenny. They were like a symbol or renewal for Jenny, a statement that they would all go forward and survive. Jenny was surprised at how proud her mother was of the books and the bookcase. It was like she hardly knew her mother at all.

Years later the bookcase still stood prominently in the front room of the flat when Jenny visited. In addition to the books originally bought there were new books on all subjects: history, novels, current events, biographies and antiques. Jenny scanned the shelf, happy the books shined so. Her mother had read every one of the books, new and old, she proudly told Jenny. Survival and growth were a part of the world that were imbedded within her family. All was well.

Afterthought:

A Neighborhood

In the traditional sense a neighborhood is a district defined in regard to its inhabitants: a fashionable place or an ethnic cluster; or a group of people who for whatever reason live in a specific place; in mathematics a set of points surrounding a specific point.

When I remember neighborhood it's more defined by the places that were within walking distance, and where when you went there you were included, not necessarily the closest place but the most accessible place.

Friendship Street was that kind of a neighborhood. There were places where we were let in, and places where we were not: our neighborhood drug store, a place that sold medicines, ice cream and soda, or lozenges for a sore throat, or aspirin, or bread and milk, wasn't physically the closest place. It was three blocks farther away from the closest drug store that was one block down and across Pine Street. Pine Street Drug had a really nice lunch counter where you could get ice cream sundaes up to the sky with whipped cream, nuts and a cherry on the top. We didn't go there, not the people from Friendship Street. Nobody knew why, or for how long the Pine Street Drug was outside the neighborhood boundary. It just was, was for a long time. That place was one that when you went there they didn't let you in. Well, maybe, the clerk might sell you a loaf of bread or a bottle of aspirin. But not without a stern look, a brusque manner that said without words you'd stepped onto the wrong stage. We wouldn't be comfortable sitting at the round red and chrome counter stools with a delicious sundae waiting for our spoons. It was an uptown store, not for the likes of us.

We knew our place and where our place wasn't. It was the adventurous or the aggressive that pushed the edges of the neighborhood map. A few of us found the better neighborhoods on long walks; we searched out college campuses or historical buildings to visit, or wandered downtown to mingle with people from the wider worlds beyond Friendship Street. We who could, who dared, learned from those sightings and moved beyond the narrow boundaries of our neighborhood, eventually away and escaped.

An afterthought: My niece Danielle was gracious and purchased this book when it was a Kindle publication. A nice book she said when we chatted about the stories. You have a great imagination, but these could not be real stories. Ah, but they were, every one, remembered and cherished. I wonder at times what happened to the players on his early stage of my life. Some I know about who had successful outcomes; some had bad ends. But mostly they have faded into the background of the scenery of Friendship Street, unknown, mostly unremembered.

About the Author.

J.M. Barry brings a multi textural background together to produce stories from a special time in American history. She has been a writer throughout her life, also a university professor, a social worker, an activist and an artisan. She uses the many shades of her own experiences to present glimpses of lives often overlooked. The author is working on additional stories from Friendship Street, and also from The Ozarks, and is completing an historical novel that will be published shortly. Presently, she and her husband live in Missouri with a good friend BEAR, a dog, Ali and a cat, Peggy, and 1000 grapevines they nurture.

The author, her Mom and sister
on Pavilion Ave 1942

www.ingramcontent.com/pod-product-compliance
Lightning Source LLC
Chambersburg PA
CBHW071227240726
48654CB00009B/951